STORM OF ROSES

A COMPILATION OF POETRY
AND SHORT STORIES

E. TARA SCURRY

Storm of Roses
A Compilation of Poetry and Short Stories, 2nd Edition
Copyright ©2021 by Ebony Tara Scurry

All rights reserved. No part of this book may be used or reproduced in any form or by any means, graphic, electronic, or mechanical, including but not limited to photocopying, recording, taping or by any information storage and retrieval system, without written permission of the Publisher, except in the case of brief quotations embodied in critical articles and reviews. Thank you for complying with copyright laws and supporting writers to continue publishing books for readers.

ISBN 978-0-578-89621-2 (Paperback)
ISBN 978-0-578-89622-9 (Ebook)

Chrysocolla Publishing
P.O. Box 4858
Silver Spring, MD 20914

Manufactured in the United States of America

*With love,
to the unforgettable memory
of my best friend
and self-proclaimed grandfather,
Mr. Lewis H. Anderson—
the most talkative, funny, caring,
and inspiring person
I've ever known.*

*How much better to get
wisdom than gold,
To choose understanding
rather than silver.*

—Proverbs 16:16

CONTENTS

Introduction 11
CHAPTER I. Light of Proverbs (Spirituality)
The Essence of God 14
Have Mercy 17
Nearer to You 19
The Carpenter 22
For You (lyrics) 24
Night Studies 25
Christian Credit Card 28
Ode to Satan: The God of This Age 32
Ode to Lucifer: The Prince of Heaven 35
Perfect Vessels To Receive 38
Blue 40

CHAPTER II. Destiny of the Breathing (Love)
Beneath the Breath of Heaven 42
Candle Love Spell 44
Doll 46
Fool 48
Heartless Dog 49
Archaic 51
Honeysuckle and Berries 53
Unique Infatuation 54
Like An Ocean 56
Mercy On Our Souls 57
My Undead Lover 58

Save My Love 60
Apple's Lover. 62
Thief 63
The Last Time I Cry 65
Third Wish. 67
With or Without 72
Confession of Unyielding love I 75
The Wine of Eternity. 77

CHAPTER III. Clenching Fists (Anger)

Deceptive Devils. 80
My Castle Is Built 81
Picking The Dead 83
Reprisal 86
Schadenfreude 87
Succumb To Nature 89
Such a Pitiful Pebble Pushed 90
Taste Your Own Toxin 91
Tired & Not Ready To Sit 92
The Fool's Concentration 94

CHAPTER IV. Elements (Earth, Wind, Fire, Water)

Women of the Sky. 98
Forbidden Underwater Palace 99
Life of the Rock 101
The Rock's Agony 102
Master of the Sun 103
Cloudburst. 104
Praise the Rays II 105
After the Rain 106
Sandy Strip of Peace 107
Earth 108
Natural Lullaby. 109
Sweet Tempest II 111
Unnatural Disaster. 113

CHAPTER V. Tears of Angels (Pain and Sorrow)

A Comfort Woman's Testimony. 116
Accept the Lies 118
Algebra is Evil 119
Alone. 120
Comfort of the Clouds 121
The Sky is Really Green 122
Lost to You 124
Not in Love 126
Numbness of Luxury. 128
Sacrilege. 129
Screwed Over in the Dark. 135
Sad Faces 136
The Light and Blades. 137
To the Light I Stumble 138
Trickling Out Over the Lovely Violets 139
Bloody White Roses 140
With Death Comes Peace 142
Double Bind 144
Ich Werde Immer Bei Dir Sein 145
Void of Essence 150

CHAPTER VI. White Hole (Miscellaneous)

Slipping 152
Clear the Way 154
The Circle 156
Elevator. 161
Destination. 165
Cream of the Crop 166
Crackhead 169
Dangerous Baby Girl. 171
A Geisha's Death in Winter 174
Blood Night 176
Naked Dance. 177
Epicurean of the Land 179
Clovers 180

  Lavender 182
  Time Alone 183
  How Good You Were 184
  Happy Moments 186
  Let the Earth Love Me II 188

CHAPTER VII. Narratives of the Wind (Short Stories & Prose)

  Banquet of Bliss. 192
  Tattoo 195
  Spark 202
  Eternity 227
  Gump Graduates 250
  Tonic Graduates. 253
  Death after the First Era: Cause and Consequence 255
  The Shrine in the Forest 287
  Storm of Roses 289

The Patty Story And Jon! And Zon (BONUS piece) 297
The Ninja Cat Irene (BONUS piece) 301
Note to Readers 303
Also by E. Tara Scurry 304
ABOUT THE AUTHOR 310

Introduction

Before I tell you what this book is about, I want to thank you. Thank you for turning these pages and for taking the time to read its contents. For years I've written poetry and stories with the hope of sharing them with the world. Your eyes on these very pages are a dream come true.

My hope is that the words and stories on the following pages cause you to second-guess your reality, question the world around you, empathize with the subject matter, know that you are not alone, challenge your current philosophy, or simply entertain you to the point of rereading the book over and over again.

Storm of Roses is about pleasure, pain, life, death, anger, spirituality, fantasies, and daydreams. The poems and stories are taken from my own experiences and beliefs or inspired by music, film, literature, current events, or the experiences of those around me.

There is a rich and irresistible freedom and permanency that comes from the written word.

Thank you for the opportunity to escort you through *Storm of Roses*.

CHAPTER I

LIGHT OF PROVERBS
(Spirituality)

The Essence of God

The image of God
is
The uniting of man and woman
Why do we call Him "he"?

You are masculine and feminine
You have a child
You are the *holy family*
The Father, the Son Jesus, and the Mother Spirit

The Father does not spare us his commands, anger, and punishment
The Son is our friend, speaking and walking with us
The Mother lays her hands on our flesh and gives peace to our souls

The Father
Jehovah
Gives us the rules of his house
He explains and is clear, we
often wish to discount those rules most difficult
especially about tithing and fornication
But there are no excuses for disobedience
He answers our questions with truth and provides for our needs
He is strong, powerful, and jealous
He demands respect and constant praise
He is a warrior, he is a protector
He is King
The Father has a vision of the big picture

He desires to give what is best for you to have
He says "No," "Yes," and "Not now" out of love
If you rebel, you regret

The Son
Jesus
Is our friend
He tells us when we are wrong, when we smell, and when
We are dirty
He is pleased with complete honesty
When we are not honest with our symptoms and sins
He knows his advice will mean nothing and withholds
Until we confess
Jesus hears our daily prayers and testifies to the Lord
When you stray from the Father's house
The Mother sends the Son to go fetch you
Jesus is hurt when you leave his side,
He is your friend who misses and worries about you
He gives you one hundred, then asks for ten back
So that he may give you two hundred, then ask for twenty
When you fight with him, he is the first to forgive
He is your conscience, keeping you from temptation and sin
He does not want you punished
by the Father's rod or drenched in the Mother's tears
Your best friend died so that you may live
He sacrificed his life, suffered false witness and torture
So that you may truly know what true friendship is

The Mother
Grace
Comforts and gives encouragement when we are weak
When our strength is dead
The Mother never gives up on her children
She is the epitome of forgiveness

The Mother monitors us as we sleep, eat, and play
Nurses us when we are sick or when our flesh is fading with illness
She patches us up when we hurt ourselves
Scolds us when we hurt others, compelling us to apologize or forgive and
To "say it like we mean it"
The Mother coaxed you back into the Father's house
when Jesus brought you to His door
when you rebelled and were reluctant with shame
Come back home, child … your Father will forgive you,
He will punish you, because We love you,
He will teach you the way, so you don't stray,
Come now, I can love you no more and no less,
She is God's Grace, affirming and giving
She praises us, spoiling us with Blessings we never deserve

Have Mercy

Merciful God
Let me please you
Let me walk by your side
Let my steps follow your steps
Take control of me

I am ill-placed
I am not of the world
Let me not be found among men
Let me faithfully serve and obey
May my attitude be of Abel
Who pleased you so greatly!
That it was your purpose for his murder
His reward it was!
That you allowed his spirit to be closer to you

Let me please you
I have faith you can seize my soul
And like Enoch
Take me away
Find me too worthy of the world
Let me be ignorant of death
And wise in you

May I please you
Every word, action, and thought
for you

Everything not of you disappears from sight
From speech
From the directions of my feet!
By your will, Lord God,
Have Mercy

CHAPTER I : Light of Proverbs (Spirituality)

Nearer to You

Heartbroken and frail
This world was meant for me
Meant to kill and drain my flesh away
Trapped and fading
Waiting
For you to take me
Diseased of my own accord and sins
He is not punishing me
Created a sinner, that I may sin
That I may punish myself because I am
Not as smart as he, not as wise as he
Created to suffer and sin against myself
Born with wants meant never to be satisfied without
guilt
Created me in flaw that I may call to him for correction
A mother who crippled her baby,
So that child may reach to be picked up
A father that burned out the eyes of his son,
That he may ask for mercy and sight
And be always dependent

Created for him, his ego
His glory, alive by his Grace

Burn out my eyes that I may appreciate my tongue?
Cripple me that I may thank you for my hands?
Distorted reasons, I cannot comprehend

What father murders one child that the other
May be more thankful for life?
I know I am filled with virus
Itching and swollen
That I may reach for your grace
To learn my body is not mine, but yours
What is this flesh but a sick
Vessel created to die?
A sinful, sick, never-satiated carcass!
Scooped into your hand, just so
I may leak through the cracks of your fingers

What is this flesh?
Why worry of the flesh?
The soul is eternal, it is gold
Flesh is dust and dirt
Heal my soul, cleanse and enliven me

As long as my spirit rests in your hand
Let my flesh do as it will
As long as my heart worships you with love
Let my flesh rot with haste, that
My soul may be that nearer to you

Why do we cling to this world?
Souls chained to dust, yearning the flesh to die
If we believed in our heavenly home
We would beg to return
And cling no longer to dirt, dust, and stone
Let my flesh rot with haste, that
My soul may be closer to you
Yes! I am filled with disease
Yes! I am filled with your Spirit
Let them both consume me

CHAPTER I : Light of Proverbs (Spirituality)

> By your grace let me die
> Quick!
> And with less suffering
> Let my flesh rot with haste, that
> My soul may be one nearer to you

The Carpenter

A young child who led and raised brows
into the world you came crying, Mary laid you in a manger
Weeping as you left, grief-stricken on the cross

Craftsman of wood with Joseph
shaping souls with God
The Lord planned for you to be a carpenter, all of your days

Sculpting spirits from painful poses into
A cup where you may live
Into a cup that the Lord may overflow with
Blessings

Distorted designs cannot catch
Blessings

Peace drains from its holes
Purpose wanders through its maze
Confused and disoriented

Master storyteller
Forming eternal life with your fingertips
Your lips
We cling to your every word, every tale
Murdered for our battle
Crucified to the voices of birds

CHAPTER I : Light of Proverbs (Spirituality)

Carpenter
May your tools rest
Besides your tomb

For You (lyrics)

You woke me up!
Your purpose is inside me, let
me do what you want me to!

I don't know what I want but
I want what you have for me
Let me live my life for your glory!

If I laugh or I cry
If hurt or I die, let
it all be for your glory!

CHAPTER I : Light of Proverbs (Spirituality)

Night Studies

Almighty Lord,
You are great and awesome
I was studying your word last eve
You were watching me
As I snuggled into the soft warmth of my bed
My sheets fluttering around me until I was comfortable
And still
My eyes rested on the book of Job

There was a day, O' Lord
You busied yourself with a wager
Why?
Satan's thoughts were not on Job
You directed Satan to him
Satan knew you would win
You knew Job would not falter
But it was worth it for Satan
In accepting your bet, he won by
Having your blessing to torment one of your children, Job
Whom he otherwise could never touch, for your protective hedge

Prompting Satan to torment your child was
Worth it to you as well
You like the recognition of being correct
Satan knew you were correct, you knew you were correct
You never tire of proving it

You never tire of hearing others say you are correct, even at
The expense or torment of your own blameless child

Poor Job!
Using him for your glory
To prove what is already known
For your upliftment, ego, and praise

We were created to be tempted
Born sinners, that no matter how upright our
Earthly life of the flesh proceeds and has been
You are always justified in punishing us or
Using us for your glory, even if it causes us pain
Because you created us guilty
Job was a human and thus a sinner
A sinner before our first word
A sinner yet on our deathbed

You have the right, Lord
Everything is yours to do as you will
If I am blessed, you will do with me as you will
As well
If it pleases you to destroy me, let me fall to pieces
If it pleases you to use me, to prove whatever you will,
Let it be done
If it pleases you to
Praise you, to demonstrate your authority,
Let it be demonstrated, your will is my prayer

Job and I are sinners
Did you allow his torment
So that you may have a reason to bless him more?
That You may take pleasure in his increased blessings
As if you never allowed his distress?
Why do you need a reason?

CHAPTER I : Light of Proverbs (Spirituality)

I ask you questions your
Word gives me answers to
But it's so strange how you are
Sometimes
You can be angry, demanding, and jealous
I am not allowed to be
But you are everything and can do anything
I will never comprehend
I was not created to understand, neither
Was Job

So I pressed my fingertips together, closing
Your word for the night
Full of more questions and fewer answers
Feeling still closer to you
The more I don't know, the more
I must trust in you

E. TARA SCURRY

Christian Credit Card

I was created blessed
I decided to cash in on some of my blessings
The other day

My feet shot across the floor as I rushed out the door
Getting to work on time
I left my lunch in the refrigerator
So much money had been saved by
Bringing and not buying my noon meal

I was so disappointed in myself!
Nature would not allow me the luxury
Of no hunger, I would have to buy today

No!
I would just eat my disheveled meal bar in my drawer and make do
Driving, quite frustrated, I prayed to the Lord to calm my heart
I hesitated to ask him to help me with
Such a silly request
But as he befriends and loves me and I submit and trust him
I grow humble and secure enough to pray for his hand in everything
No matter how small or apparently trivial
Then I began, as humble and faithful as I could

CHAPTER I : Light of Proverbs (Spirituality)

I know you will provide for me today
Please Lord; take my hunger away when the time comes
May a coworker be so kind as to take me out for lunch
Please, Lord, it's out of my hands; I give this situation to you
I need you to take it from me; you promised to provide
Let your will be done; take control Lord Jesus
Please provide for me today, Lord; no one is as merciful as you

I'm at work, at my desk; it's 12:04 and I'm hungry
The phone rings, I pick up
Hello, Human Resources!
Yes, may I speak to Ms. Scurry?
This is she; may I help you?
This is Domino's. You ordered a pizza from us last week
Yes, I did ...
I was calling to ask how you felt about the quality of our service
It was wonderful! But one of the pizzas was half pepperoni instead of half cheese
Why didn't you call us? We don't want you to be dissatisfied!
It wasn't a big deal; the other pizza was okay. It wasn't that important
No, it is to us! I'm sending you a large pizza right now! What do you want to drink?
Huh? Well ... how about pineapple, tomato ... wow, this is amazing!
Okay, do you like chicken wings?
I don't eat chicken ... a large is too big ... for real? Some Sprite. Oh! Thank you so much!
It's on its way; please call us next time if there is any mistake
Wow, you know, I forgot my lunch this morning and I prayed in my car for like eight Minutes asking God to provide my lunch for me today! This is amazing!
Are you a Christian?

Yes, and see, this is just amazing ... oh my goodness! He is so awesome!
I'm glad to be of service, that's pretty cool, have a great day
Oh, thank you so much! Bye!

I rested the phone on its base
And let tears fall from my face
Oh how God provides
Much more than we ever need

I ate pizza that day and the next day and still had enough to share
The six-pack of Sprite, more than enough
I did, however, manage to refuse the chicken
With such blessings overflowing in abundance
I could not even catch them all

As Rev. Price would say
We are already blessed
Prayer is the credit card number and
Jesus is the password

I bask in the blessings he so mercifully provides
Oh if He would intertwine in the small parts and
The large parts, and just every part of
My life

Let me trust you and willingly give you the reins!
That you may cover and take care of me
That I may praise and honor you
Because you work!
You are for real!
Because I am never going back to being without you!
I don't see how I've come this far
Ah ha! But only by your mercy was it so
And only by your mercy may it never be so again!

CHAPTER I : Light of Proverbs (Spirituality)

With God you must believe it before you see it
A part of us must die before we can truly live
You must seek of your own accord to learn more about him
Then he will scoop you up! So fast! Questions, curiosity, and doubt
Bring you closer, not farther from him
Don't be afraid of the unknown
He has always known you and knows you still
He doesn't want to be an acquaintance; he wants to be a friend
It is that he wants you
To know him!
Because he wants you to ask questions
That he may enjoy your conversing and relationship (Don't you feel
good when someone's interested in you too?)
Because he wants you to be curious
That you will study his word and fellowship with others curious
like you, evenly yoked!
Because he wants you to doubt
That you may learn of faith, trust, and prayer, so he may bless you
And you see with your own flesh
Feel with your spirit, that his promises to you are fulfilled before
You even ask, before you even know what you need

Blessings are there, waiting for you
Limitless, don't miss them
Cash them out, for there are plenty more in Heaven still
Waiting for you
Waiting for you

Ode to Satan: The God of This Age

Bold and fiery dragon
Accuser of the brethren
Evil one
Tempter
All these you are
Only the ignorant and those apathetic to truth
Know you as Lucifer, that prosperous mistranslated myth

All things were created by God
You are a spirit, not a thing and physical
God saw everything he created; it was good
You are the epitome of evil
God created the heavens and the earth
The Word does not say God
Created the heavens, the earth, and hell
I will not believe what the Word does not say
I will not infer, assume, or add

But you, King of Demons
Powerful and heavy on our backs
Make mothers murder their babies
Fathers kill themselves from the inside out
Children bludgeon children

Only you
Are given such rein and authority
To dare go against the desires of God
To his very face
You have been in his mighty presence
How bold you are!

Impressive lying wonders and gifts the
Flesh truly appreciate
When we ask of you, immediately you answer
When I ask for your sweet wicked delights
Unlike the Lord, you never refuse me
You embrace and answer my prayers for the present
You never make me wait for your aid
You are on a timetable; God is not

Who are you, Satan?
God did not create you or hell
He does not mention your origin
But fills pages only on how to resist you, as if
Knowing that is more important than knowing your birth
Or the origin of hell since he
Created only the heavens and earth

Are you the personification of sin and wickedness
Or are you truly a spiritual entity?
I believe
You are a powerful, bold, and feeling spiritual being
For the Devil led Jesus to a high place to tempt him with
The kingdoms of the world
Sin did not lead Jesus
The Devil led Jesus to Jerusalem
Wickedness did not lead Jesus

God loves me, sin after sin
Despite my sins
You embrace me, sin after sin
Because of my sins

God created us as sinners from the womb
With you, I can be myself, as I was born to be
A sinner from the womb
You take me as I am
I am always welcome and greeted with enthusiasm

God makes me change before
I am welcome in his palace
I must take off my shoes
Clean my flesh and
Brush up my faith
With you
I can come as I am

Ode to Lucifer: The Prince of Heaven

Lucifer, bright and beautiful
I believe your story
I will believe it all my life and not diverge

Such a powerful, emotional, and handsome Cherub
You always had the utmost authority and privilege
You were the loving and loyal
Right Hand of God
Before Jesus was even a plan
When God rested on the seventh day
You faithfully looked after his estate with care

How God cheated you, the most faithful
The one most truly like God
Eldest Son and Friend
The Prince of Heaven
By giving dominion of the new and great creation
Earth
To man instead of the angels
Instead of you!

Oh how God showered Adam and Eve with affection!
How he relentlessly loved and interacted with the world
The attentions of your brothers no longer
A priority

And what would I do, Lucifer
But be twisted with jealousy and confusion?
As you ran the affairs of heaven while He
Preoccupied and lost in thought
Gazed with excitement and wonder
Into the glass tank, every moment watching
His new creation vibrate, move, and grow
Realigning and editing his exhilarating masterpiece!
Like Jacob, God clothed us with elaborate robes
Showered us with relentless favoritism
Because he is king and the head of his house
We serve God; he is our customer
And he is always right
And you are truly his Eldest Son
Inheritor of your father's intense jealousy
And what then, Lucifer?
Like the elder brothers of Joseph, you wished us dead

I understand your story
No matter how perfect and faithful you were
God's attention lacked what it had been
Until you manipulated his new joy
In an effort to showcase our inherent imperfection
That God would destroy us for our sin and embrace you
But alas, in anger he tossed *you* out
Your anger and need for love and attention
Eternally
Inflamed

And what madness would I succumb to, Lucifer
If the eyes of the Lord were to turn from me?
Would I not know pure misery too?
Every time you pull at us, you have God's full attention
Do you not?

You and your jealous angels remain envious
Coveting the attention we receive
When will you and God reconcile?

When you accept the slight of your birthright?

When will God finally give
His Eldest son
His rightful inheritance?

Perfect Vessels To Receive

I love you
I want you to love as I do
This is why in my every action
I thought of you, that I
Would serve as an example to you

It warms my heart to hear you sing to me
To clap, smile, and dance in my name
To eat bread and drink wine in remembrance

Who that you know would say
To your face
That they would die for you?
I say it, looking into your eyes
Every time you turn the pages of our Father's Word

How I love you,
How I know the power of actions
So I suffered and bled for you
I hung hungry, weak, and wet with blood
Sticking to my flesh
I died for you

Because you are imperfect
You are perfect vessels to receive my love
Angels holy and perfect don't capture the love
And attention that you draw out of me

CHAPTER I : Light of Proverbs (Spirituality)

I am drawn to the needy
I am drawn to the disheveled and abused
I am drawn to pain, imperfect flesh, and tainted hearts
I am a social worker of souls

I argue for your sake and listen to your woes
I do not blame the victim; you are good
It is evil and the ways of the world which warp you
From your original design

I am a carpenter; let me carve you into a holy shape
With less flesh and more spirit
And humble yourself small that I may be able to carry you

Do you love me because I give you greater purpose?
But I love you the same, for what purpose is greater than giving
Love?
For what purpose is greater than giving
Life?

Blue

The night sky is blue
Navy blue
With deep rounds of rough wool

Scattered along the earth are careless
Patches of light
Those who close their eyes but do not sleep
Who lay their cheeks against soft pillows
But do not rest
Their flesh is awake
Bodies ache and minds worry
Thin, malnourished souls
Some anorexic, many bulimic
Some fat and sick with junk and sweets

The night is black
Blue-black
It is dark and they cannot see
They can hear but cannot understand
They must reach out to feel their way
Blind, disoriented
Because there is no light
Inside them
To guide them

CHAPTER II

DESTINY OF THE BREATHING
(Love)

Beneath the Breath of Heaven

Down like your tears
We will fall
Not in vain like the shining sun
On seedless soil
Fall, fall for me
For us, fall with the passion of
Thousands of tears twisted
From the ocean's eyes
Its turbulent seas

Chimes
It is the wind
We are strong
Get your feet wet, sink
My precious lover

Fall with me onto knees
Beneath the breath of heaven
Fall into the merciless waters
We will breathe the breath of heaven
Peace in the icy seas
Sink silently, surrounded by wild sea flowers

I've found the secret path
Silver lights strike our eyes
In the peaceful icy seas, light glows
Only in the coolness of the waters
Is the embrace of my arms appreciated

Sink with me, breathe with me
The path is deep
Immortal
Bright and peaceful like an angel
Fragrant and lovely like a hill of tulips
Even in the thick liquid of the icy seas

Candle Love Spell

You will come back to me; my hand is in the magical air
You cannot resist your five senses
The elements will pull you to me
Like rain to the flowers of the earth
You will water my desires
You are pure, wet, and weak now
Fall from the clouds of my candle's smoke
I'll drink you forever

Mold you to my pleasure
You'll chase after me like
The light is destined to chase the night
You'll stick to me like
The scent of a flower

Rose quartz stones
Candles of red, white, and pink
The shadow of my obsession
Forces you to realize now
Because my hands are in the magical air
You're engraved toward your destiny
Don't fight, just come
My candle's light will guide you
Through the dark and confusion's reflections
Be comfortable on your knees
I won't let them bruise
On a soft fur carpet you will kneel
But kneel you shall

CHAPTER II : Destiny of the Breathing (Love)

I love you with a terrible love
You've been bewitched by elements' mercy
My hands are in the magical air
You're engraved toward your destiny
You'll be he who stares with obsession
Eyes glazed over with incomprehensible love
It is I who shall smile and know how we came to be
It is I who shall smile and know why you can never be free of me
My intentions are pure and true
That I'll be forever with you
No one is better for you than me
I'm doing you a favor by enslaving you
Chains of love, cages of love
And you, my love
Are engraved toward your destiny
Stop fighting, just come
The light of my candle will guide you
Through the dark and confusions' reflections
Be comfortable on your knees
I won't let them to bruise
On a soft fur carpet you'll kneel
But kneel you shall

I love you with a terrible love
My intentions are pure and true
That I'll be forever with you
I am the only one who
Truly loves you

Doll

I was thrown
Tossed to the side
Glass eyes

I was used
Now I'm lost
Among his other dolls
In my little dress

He could have put me
Back on the shelf neatly
But I was cast back
I'm not even sitting straight
With my legs twisted,
My arm curled under me,
Head hanging to the side
I hate the way I look like this
Lifeless, deprived, worn

It's obvious to me
I am his doll
I was played with
I am old
He has a new doll
She's young and beautiful
Her dress isn't ragged like mine
I am of the old trend

CHAPTER II : Destiny of the Breathing (Love)

I am an old toy
My parts creak
I kiss dust
Instead of his lips

As the days go by
I'm even less desirable
Dress turning gray
Dirt in my hair
And he doesn't even care
Why would he or anyone
Ever want to pick me up again?

I am a doll
Just a toy, turned off
My time is over, batteries dead
Expiration date, here
Now

No one will ever touch my hair again
No one will ever make me dance
No one will ever kiss my cheek as he
I am not alone, but I am by myself
On this shelf, away from his heart

Fool

i am a fool
Because i believed in you
i am a fool
Because i still want you
i am a fool
that's why you forgot me
i am a fool
Because i'll love you forever

CHAPTER II : Destiny of the Breathing (Love)

Heartless Dog

You're drinking me like liquor
How do you feel?
Do I heat your temper
And create a fire in your throat?
Do you cough up air violently
As you cough up lies?

I've got to clot the blood of my pain
From which you've drained
From which you twisted my love
Until you seeped all you could
Each drop forced out
Against my will, against my honor
You left me
Empty, weak, and withered
And the worst
You left me
Without your love
To refill my heart you've milked

I'm cold in my loneliness
Without you
And you're enjoying
Every moment we're apart
Ravishing my heart so I'll cry more sweet tears

You're drunk off my begging
You lap hungrily at the nectar of my pain
You heartless dog
You beast
You devil
My love

CHAPTER II : Destiny of the Breathing (Love)

Archaic

Prelude:
I was a tree and selfish with the rain given to me
He grew brown and dry, breaking off away from me
Before he even touched the ground
The wind had picked him up and carried him far away

He was my air
He was my soul
He was every breath inside of me

He watered my fears
And every free moment when day is alive
I see his eyes, feel the pang of loss
Even dark shadows of sleep refuse to shield me
From painful and beautiful recollections

He's in my eyes
He's in my hands
Though time dwindles
My love never decays

Yet is it impossible for him to
Take me again, into his heart?
I will try
I will answer my own questions

He is my blood
He is my only regret
I was foolish to let him slip from my tender clutch
He's running free, dodging my grasps
I am growing tired
Yet my will is just as strong
As my desire to express my love to him, forever
And my life isn't over yet
Neither is my hope

CHAPTER II : Destiny of the Breathing (Love)

Honeysuckle and Berries

She is soft
Like the petals of a rose
She is fresh like the fields
On a spring day at noon

She is smart, nice, and lovely
I want to pet her
Her locks of hair play tag
With the creamy gentleness of her shoulders
I want to breathe her
I want to affect her
Because she is soft like me
And she smells of honeysuckle and berries

If she would only rest on a silky bed of flowers
Smile brightly and talk nonsense
It would make the loveliest picture
For my heart, forever

This unborn scene, this aromatic notion
Makes me want to breathe her
I want to impress her
Because she is soft like me
And smells of honeysuckle and berries

Unique Infatuation

Your power is so immense
I've overflowed
Short-circuited
My engine has died
But like a car to a tow
I remain anchored to you
Moving after you
Not by my own feet but
By the power within you
Magnetic
Electric energy
Moving after you
Daydreaming of you
Night-wishing for you

A beer in your left, vodka in your right
Such filthy words you say
Curse here, curse there, spitting over there
Full of hiccups
Yet it doesn't bother me at all
You are so immense
My spirit aches to know you
My heart knows where you stand
But has no base of its own

CHAPTER II : Destiny of the Breathing (Love)

Such a strange manner
I am drawn to you because
First you drew to me, then away
Like an insect to a light, touching and going
Touching and going

I am too lovely to wait for you
I am not too proud to wish for you
I've already drifted in love with your honesty
Thank you

My dreams and wishes will come to pass
When
The time is right
Now

When your voice calls me sweetheart
I become warm and supple
When my fingers travel over your brown locks
Pushing them away from your brown eyes
I know you like it
You told me so
What else do you like?
My spirit aches to know you!
My heart knows where you stand
But has no base of its own

Friends and admirers scattered about you
Like grass at your feet
You are no man
But untamed and unique

E. TARA SCURRY

Like An Ocean

True love is like an ocean
It can crash viciously against the small and unarmed sand
It can sweat like passion and glisten off the rocks with the heated warmth of the sun
It can rest peacefully in the gentleness beneath the cool breath of the moon
You can play in it or let it drown you before you've realized you've sunk into its depths

CHAPTER II : Destiny of the Breathing (Love)

Mercy On Our Souls

Favored we are for
When I cry, you are aware
When I die, you will feel it
Unconditionally love me, have me
Now and for eternity you will be with me
Your promises, priceless
Like the golden apples of heaven
So sweet my tears are to your
Fingertips

Kissing these quivering and forlorn lips
Loving this morose and weary woman
Looking so far out into forthcoming suns
That the present is blurry and I struggle
To embrace it
In my slippery and fragile fingers

My depressed and anxious psyche remains
Frail while this heart
Never falters and knows no illness
We are favored in the eyes of Time
It heals, reinforces, and strengthens us
Let it continue to have mercy on our souls
Let it continue to have mercy

E. TARA SCURRY

My Undead Lover

He was my sky and I were his clouds
Strangers envied us, the perfect youthful pair
As we held souls only under the night's sky
Not soon, time scraped the youth from my skin
These same strangers began to stare
I could read their eyes, *That woman couldn't be his grandmother,
kissing his lips thus*
*And she's much too old, and especially a woman, to be paired with
such a handsome man. She must be rich*

I grew weary of the looks and painful whispers
And it hurt because my lover never wrinkled like my own flesh
I tried to push him, fight him away
But he would not leave my side
When I ran, he would find me
When I would yell, he would kiss the screams away as well
He would not let me throw him aside

I never needed anything or anyone except him
Very old now; his strong arms were my cane
His love cured any physical or emotional ill
I grew frailer and deathly weak, on this thin white mattress
I'm one hundred and twelve years old
Never even once did he refuse me anything
Now, I'm merely a shell on a cloth in this dry and sterile building

CHAPTER II : Destiny of the Breathing (Love)

As my soul rises slowly in waves from my body
Like smoke after a flame
I can still see him near my flesh
He's always been older and wiser in age
He's always had the exact body of the young man I'd first met
I see his hand holding the thin hand of my body
And for once, it is as cold as his

I am about to leave this room
I panic suddenly, because I will lose his face from my eyes
His head spins around and he looks up at me
Or through me, past my spirit
Dark crimson tears fall from his eyes
His pale, unlined face seemed blushed with anguish suddenly
If I could cry then, I did
If I could reach out to him, I did also

I am going to a palace of white crystal and golden gates
Will his mysterious soul ever be allowed to come with me?
When his eternity ends, will he be returned to me
And be my dark angel within Heaven's light?

Save My Love

No matter how many years go by
We will never know our tomorrow
You are still locked away in thoughts
Epitome of regret
My soul mate forever
Severed
Will my shames ever pass from me?
Forgive me, please
Know not, I did
That when I stepped into the four winds
I stole a piece of each of our souls
And sent them into the belly of the flame

Satisfaction we might taste on
Another love's lips
Yet fulfillment shall never
Grow within a new heart's beat

Maybe on our deathbed
We may return our pieces
One
Maybe angels will
Cry for our story
From whose roots miracles may grow

CHAPTER II : Destiny of the Breathing (Love)

    Busy those white wings are
   Catching falls and blocking bullets
    But what is the worth of life
      Without love?

     Come now, angel,
     Guardian angel
    Catch my mistakes and
   Set them upright once more
     Save my life
     Save our love

Apple's Lover

I'm a Golden Delicious apple
And if you bite into me
It'll sound like you're stepping on rocks
My perfumed juices will dribble
Down past your lips
Making flat spheres on your chin

Even after you've had your fill
My tender sticky essences will linger
Your tongue will lap upon my sweetness
My aftermath will shine like gloss
Signaling to all
You're mine

CHAPTER II : Destiny of the Breathing (Love)

Thief

Stole my love
A man once tall and beautiful
Lied to yourself about what you had
And gave it to me

Lies dribbling down the sides of your mouth
Deception in your eyes
What a fool I was to believe
You trusted yourself

You are black and white
Beautiful on the outside
Ugly on the inside
Dipped in guilt, only God can rinse you
You ask him, fingers crossed behind your back
Picking and choosing which words of his
You will obey
Picking and choosing which lies you will tell me today

Left me more than brokenhearted
Left me with your illness
I refused to take your self-denial
There I am wiser than you

The first was the worst, with another love
The second, I was too numb to feel damage
With you I knew how it felt

To have a sour and rotting heart of stink
Only the promises of God could maintain
My sanity and routine

No hate for you here
I pray every day that God bless me with a peaceful
And loving attitude, to take any bitterness and blame away
So good is God to me
He healed my body
Despite doctor's speech

My precious lover, the thief
Lies from your mouth, lies from your actions
Lies ahead of you and behind
They are rising, surrounding
You see them, eye level
Rising above you, lift your head up
Then drown, feet kicking hands scratching

Let your dead body float
Bloated with lies, surrounded with lies
Buried in a sea of lies
Slimy scavengers of the deep don't want you
Neither do I
They nibble once at your dirty, sickly flesh, then swim away
Dirty, sickly, full of lies
The ugliest person I've known deep inside
I do not miss your warmth and comfort
I do not miss your gentle lies and fake hopeful stories

Go
Go float
Go float far
Far away from me

CHAPTER II : Destiny of the Breathing (Love)

The Last Time I Cry

For the past couple of months
I have been preoccupied
Because my lover had gone astray
Because I had pushed him away
Every second and every day
Memories of us beat loudly on my doors
When I went to open them, they disappeared
They haunted me ruthlessly

I could not seem to let him go
I was in love
Somewhere inside me
I still felt he loved me too

Peace would never restrain my longing
I must call him back to me
I could not rest until I could say,
I tried
And so with every ounce in me
And with each breath I inhaled
Day by day and night to night
I fought for us

Woe it will be
If it shall come to pass
That my lover refused my hand
I, in turn, must understand

The lights will fade
The fire frozen and broken
Like the sweet promises he spilt
Time and love expired

Sadness will kiss me
My new lover shall be agony
I will make love with my own tears
Under my sheets, on my pillow, and
In the darkness of night

But those tears must stop
And I shall breathe again
Life will continue
And so shall I
Thus, this is it
If he pinches out the flame
I can still be at peace
For I know I tried my best

I pray
Let him accept my love
So I may live in its heat and shine with him

An end or a new beginning
No matter, here the pain must rest
This is where the agony must die
The last time I cry

CHAPTER II : Destiny of the Breathing (Love)

Third Wish

If I had three wishes
I'd secure my place in Heaven
Next to my grandfather, the soldier
With the belly and gray hair
Then I'd wish for universal environmental peace
Encompassing each planet
Finally
I'd ask for you

I don't know you
Never touched my hand to yours
But I've seen you
Albeit not with my own eyes
But through the screen
I know you, everyone does
The sexy celebrity
But not you, the person
So I really don't know you

Similar to the celebrity
But deeper and different
I'm not so ignorant
To tumble in obsession with an image
A mere projection of who you are
The creation of what you want others
To think you are

I admire your star, the celebrity
I am enthralled with the person
I think you might be underneath
Or is that too ignorant of me?
To think that I might find who you really are
More pleasing than
Who you want me to think you are
Me and the world
But I don't want the star; he's too perfect for me
I prefer something real and flavorful
With flaws and the occasional bad mood

The celebrity smiles, signs photos, and gives
Group hugs
He is appreciative, sometimes humbled and
Often overwhelmed, always surrounded
The person is writing at his desk
Walking around his huge house
His dogs following in stride
Or away in a home not his own
Filming
But alone
Imperfect
Human
Desiring the type of companionship that carries no tag
That's what makes us beautiful and real
Our imperfect flesh and personalities
The reiteration that things most valuable
Cannot be bought

Universal desires
On this we are all equal
We both know your money can provide
Pleasant distractions if you care to have them

CHAPTER II : Destiny of the Breathing (Love)

Let me tell you, please
It's like sleeping when you're hungry
When your eyes finally open
You see only hunger before you
And sometimes it's bold enough to disturb
Your very dreams

Life is easier for you
Because of who people think you are
But love, relationships
So, so much more difficult
People who have hands to hold
Look at you and want your money
Fame, your star
And you may look back at them
And want hands to hold

Someone to love
Enough to trust and
Have your babies
You value marriage and believe in it
You wish to hold your own child
Yours
Not only your tiny precious costars
I wish you well
Sincerely I do
You've done such great things
I know there's more to come
Love doesn't consume itself over money
It makes age obsolete
It makes race trivial
You, who refuse to cleave to any
One race
It's beautiful, your methods

Love, it latches
On similarities and grows on the delicate
Balance
Of mutual compensation for strengths and weaknesses

If you ever come to D.C.
For an interview or premiere
Call on me
If your person is a gentleman
I may provide pleasant company
For dinner (or what have you, but I most enjoy activities involving food)
If my schedule permits
If you come, bring yourself
And if you don't, I'll know
If you open the car door for me
It's you
If your driver opens it
The star is blinding my eyes
And I'll look on someone else
Who I can see without wincing

Though, I can't resist adding—Instead of saying,
"Thank you for dinner. I had a really good time! Good night."
I'll say,
"Thank you for dinner. I appreciate it! Take care."
(And don't ask a woman if she had a good time. She'll tell you. If she doesn't, you don't want to know. If you ask, she may not tell the truth if she values not hurting your feelings over honesty.)

You could be very comfortable as an actor
But insist on stepping out
Of your comfort zone and into your dream
I admire that and believe in your ability

CHAPTER II : Destiny of the Breathing (Love)

It could be a pleasure to make your acquaintance
If, most importantly, he is a gentleman
But remember,
Your soul mate will never look
Or be
How or who you imagined
So do as you will
You've taken many chances; what's one more?
What do you have to lose besides
Your soul mate
Relax and don't assume
Is your lucky number really 40?
Take as much time as you need
Take risks, take a chance
You've done well by them so far

E. TARA SCURRY

With or Without

I'm young
Some ask why I'm
Single
Some ask why I'm not
Married
Age has nothing to do with it

I respect marriage
I value it
I respect others' marriages
When or if I get married, I'll respect mine
If I get married, it will be forever
It's a serious, life-changing, and lifelong commitment
I take it very seriously
Thank goodness it's the man who has to ask
My daddy
If a man asks me, my first question back is,
What did my father say?
If you haven't asked him,
I can only tell you *no*
If he's given you permission
I can say *yes* or *no*

My parents have been married for over thirty-five years
Yes, they fuss and all
But I don't think it's because they've been married for so long
It's just because they're o—

CHAPTER II : Destiny of the Breathing (Love)

I mean, *becoming more senior*
All seniors fuss a lot
Amongst themselves, married or not
God has blessed old married people, though
He blesses them with short-term memory lapses
So they forget what they fought about yesterday
Stay together year after year
Remembering only the good from the past
That brought them together

I like being alone
I like having a refrigerator filled
With my "unmeat/funny-food/bootleg-chicken," organic and soy
Without complaint
Wearing sheer and short nightgowns without a robe
I like a lot of things about being by myself
Marriage would have to make my life a lot better than it is
Not simply a little happier or better, not even the same

Why do people think the fun stops when you marry?
You can still go to the club, party, and travel
With your husband
At least that's what I heard

But I do know that
I want to go snowboarding
And then come inside the warm chalet
And start making babies
Couple years later come back, go snowboarding with the kids
Come inside the warm chalet
Watch movies with the kids, play board games
Put them to bed
And make more babies
I can do all that by myself or with friends

Except the baby-making part, anyway
And I will and have a blast

I respect marriage
I value and believe
It is a good thing
I don't think it's for everyone
And it may not be for me
I don't know what the future holds
But I know what I'm going to make
Of my future
With or without someone else

CHAPTER II : Destiny of the Breathing (Love)

Confession of unyielding love I
(Taken from T.O.E.: Book II)

I miss you so much
Like I can't breathe
I dream you are here
Warm next to me
No pain, no wrongs

We breathe hope into our lungs and live
Why us? Why must fate swat, bite, and batter us?
Like a cat to a mouse, not dead but wounded and bleeding
You're the only thing that's ever felt unmistakably right
Nothing so right can be wrong
No matter what they say
No matter how much they beat me
Beat us

I see nothing but you
I will feel nothing but you
Let them hit me; I care of nothing
But being with you
You are everything to me

E. TARA SCURRY

A part of me rests in you
I am not right when away from you
I need you like the flowers need the sun
I am wilting, dying, and cold without you
I need you like a fish needs the sea
Suffocating and helpless
Wanting the only thing that can keep me alive
The heat by which you touch me
The air of your presence I breathe
That keeps me alive
I need you
I have to be with you
Or I swear, I will die

CHAPTER II : Destiny of the Breathing (Love)

The Wine of Eternity

Before you even finish telling your woes,
I'm already wiping your tears
Before you even finish the whispers of my name,
I'm already by your side
To aid, comfort, and love
You see, my love isn't just love
My love is so true, it never blinds me
In truth, I have never before seen so clearly
Through life's fog or confusions

You see, I will love you
Beyond the end of time
I will beg for your soul, in Heaven
No tears are allowed in God's palace
Yet I will cry out with my tongue
And shed the sorrow of my soul
If God does not give you to me
I will say, *his soul is my soul*
Accept me, Lord, and he must be accepted too for we are one
And cannot be without the other. If he must go to Hell,
Let me remain at his side. he is my joy in
Both darkness and light
I will not cease until the winged ones unlock your chains
Or chain me, to go below with you

Let us say God let you out to join me
As I would walk with you now
To our new home in heaven
Where the flowers shine like small stars
And the golden streets are bright with gold
I would think back to mortality
And how, in our past, we wronged each other
Yet love is the greatest forgiver
And we forgave, and here we are after death
Now, and truly alive
Our souls literally kiss
This is the wine of eternity
We shall drink, drink, and drink
I have never known happiness such as
These long priceless moments in heaven with you
But I am not dead yet
So I pray and cry that we die

CHAPTER III

CLENCHING FISTS
(Anger)

Deceptive Devils

Why am I so disappointed?
Is that even the right word, or is
Angry
More appropriate?
It is not all right
I am not fine either
Something is wrong, but
I can't pinpoint it
I do know that it is
Festering
In the pit of my heart
Shadowed by a multitude
Of something I may never understand

I'm weak with delirium
Slipping over the wet sadness
That sneaks past my strength and falls in tears from my eyes
Can anyone be authentic?
Who will remain cemented in truth?
You've all done wrong by me

Don't set me up, just look
Haven't you done enough?
I'm disappointment's evaporation
A contorted shell withered and left behind
I am overwhelmed with all of you

CHAPTER III : Clenching Fists (Anger)

My Castle Is Built

I do as I please
Say I can't
If it's good for me
I will
I will be mistaken
Get over it

My future is in my hands
Dig my own grave
Build my own castle
I will be mistaken
You say, an overachiever
I'd rather have a castle
Where one end is unseen from the other
Than a shack where
One must wipe her feet before going
Outside

Don't waste your time
Lashing vicious names with jealousy's tongue
You're already behind
Fate grabs at your ugly ankles
Swollen from standing in place
Fat with fake gratification

Tame me, my aspirations?
I will drink my fill of opportunities
Call me a shrew
But I've got an
Education
And hips

Whipping your own back
Standing in place
Trying to divert me
You remain still
Other times
You're foolish enough to run backwards
Tripping over yourself because you can't see
While I move on to important things
So keep digging your hole
Until it's dark and cold
Until the sand falls around and over you
Until you suffocate in your foolishness and die by yourself

CHAPTER III : Clenching Fists (Anger)

Picking The Dead

Let's see you
Blood shining off the cracked mirror
Your bones scraping my plate
This is the last time I'll forgive you
Just keep wiping me on the cold rocks
There can be no more
I can only absorb so many welts
Until I collapse
Come into my black hole

You will see a side unknown to you
Chop the flower down, grow a knife anew

Come find Hell with me
I won't stop until I see it all
That evil being turned, inside out
I'm caged in, pouring out this agony
I was compelled to let it go,
Because God handles everything
Yet, as you kept picking the dead
You couldn't raise them up

The clouds opened their arms to me
And I swam in the new revelation
That this Lord sends her angels
To press her will upon her subjects
And thus, I send myself
It must come to an end, the eternal nightmare

This eve, I am convinced
That I alone have the permission
Of the Mighty Hand
And she says in her heated selflessness,
Fallen leaf, do as you will

My smile never faded
And then, you kept pushing me
Unstringing my tight corset of control
Here now, you have that which was asked
Is this your true desire?
A crazed and wicked angel, unable to fly
Yet I've spread my wings, confident
I never forgot your bestialities
I'm on my mission

This is the last you will see of my previous self
My smile still here, permanently embedded onto my face
There are volcanoes in my nerves
I will lash out at your nefarious evil
I love you, but it is a necessity
Must love my neighbor and the stranger
Must love the enemy as my friend
Despite the rules, as all beautiful angels in the sky
Some are destined to feel blood on their fingertips

I've turned the other cheek for you
As instructed by her
And you took it again and again
I have nowhere else to step
My ground is covered with oil
The slickness of my inner turmoil
Came alive when you pricked my soul
Leaking me empty, all over the earth

CHAPTER III : Clenching Fists (Anger)

Growing mold of my frustration
Nothing left for you to defile, it's over
The true royalty of divine doormats
Rubbed under the filthy heel of my boot
Bludgeoned under the burden of my sword

Reprisal

Loud yet invisible
The sun shining in my face
Idiots refuse to kneel in my grace
My wrath is too mystical for ignorance
So the earth turns, the sky bleeds
The trees sway in their meekness
All my life runs out of me
The walls squeeze my soul, it hurts
My body melts, my skin's on fire
Only thing worse is my desire
To see you lying in the grave
So still, unable to torture me anymore

Beyond the mountain and the lake
Lies the truth which you forsake
And on that day, you will come to me
Striking vainly with your blasphemy

CHAPTER III : Clenching Fists (Anger)

Schadenfreude

I have thin strings for arms
How could I do anyone harm?
I need to see the sky, but I cannot see that high
Can someone come down to me
And tell me how I should be
Gib mir kraft

I have all this grief inside
I want to twist and turn and cry
I want to see you folded between two walls of needles
Smothered by your own mischievous spirits
I want to hear your cries
As your screams compress alongside your insides
Gib mir kraft

That feeling, which I will get
As I eat of your seasoned flesh
And drink of your fresh sweetened blood
Eating and digesting you
Destroying you inside myself, passing through
Like the waste you are
That feeling, that gift
Gib mir kraft

I have never had the luxury of pleasure
I know not the relief of a hug
I never had anyone to give me love
I am just a little piece of dirt
Gib mir kraft

But now I know Schadenfreude
The pleasure and quickening of my skin
When I feel your blood splatter
Like the rain of a thousand tears
Like the sweet wickedness of a thousand illicit crimes
That feeling, the gift
Schadenfreude
Give me strength

CHAPTER III : Clenching Fists (Anger)

Succumb To Nature

Slip, fall, collapse
Maybe perhaps
You can save me
But you won't
It's your own trap
That's locking me down
But my voice makes no sound
Because you've rendered it useless
I'm invisible,
I'm so miserable
But this is the way it has to be

The courage I had withered and fell
Almost as quick as you can spell
Pathetic
At least I can say I tried, but I lack fortitude
So I conceal this deficiency
From myself and from you
From this horrifying polluted earth
But this is the way it has to be

Just dare to breathe a gentle evil word
You'll watch me succumb to nature
Like the dead and crackled leaves of fall
But I'll descend awkwardly like the rain
Quiet like the snow and with my eyes blazing like the sun
Everything falls: the rain, snow, and sunshine
Who have no choice but to submit to their fate
Neither do I

Such a Pitiful Pebble Pushed

In bloom I'll grow
Then no more will your lies
Continue to molest my insides
I have no more worries

You're like the pebble that's been displaced
By the rough wind's sour breath
It was the ultimate sin to hurt me
You'll reap your own viciousness
I swear it

Such a pitiful pebble pushed
Along the cold waters of my lake
Forced over and wet with my sobbing
Down the waterfall, the pebble cracks
Like my smile when I see you bleed

CHAPTER III : Clenching Fists (Anger)

Taste Your Own Toxin

I want to poison you
So you'll die
I want to be the last one you see
Before you close your eyes
Don't ask me why
Because I won't tell you
I want you to die
Full of questions
Like my life was
With you

E. TARA SCURRY

Tired & Not Ready To Sit

Heated pot
Slowly simmers
Looks calm
Time is cruel
Thinking that Time
Lays low lame lies
Far from eyes
Under feet

Wounds cover over with the hours
In casket in the dark
Scars still seem the same as they were
Never gone
Only then decay with the rest of the flesh
By then, soul is far away

Nothing in this realm can be discarded
Let go pain, love, worldly success, guilt
But look there in your hand
Imprint indented illegibly in hands
Cannot read it, only feel it there
Even though you let it go

CHAPTER III : Clenching Fists (Anger)

Brutal is time
Like the devil,
Misrepresenting himself
With ourselves in the dark
Never alone
All of our pain, love, worldly success, guilt
Memories

Cruel music implanted in our ears
Cannot change station
Imprinted hands fumble in the dark
Walking the earth then
With terrible dances and strange beats
Decaying on the earth
Dancing sadly to loud music

When Rest comes to tap our shoulders
In black cape and tall staff
The first quiet; stillness of limbs as we find our seats
Sitting down, flesh will slither and fall off its bones under us
Like a ball and chain to the ground
Touching the legs of the chairs
Red, white, and pink fleshy tissue
Skeleton in seat
Cruel haunted jokes of Time

No choice but to listen
To bellyfuls of foul laughing
No choice but to listen
To sad loud music

E. TARA SCURRY

The Fool's Concentration

I've picked the lock on these cuffs
Let the hour come when you are ready
To peel the layers of my spirit
You will find nothing of use or value
I won't be there for you now, not anymore
So just cling tightly to your foolish loitering

I would have staggered out of this misery
To better and less simple things
To resourceful and less selfish men
Departing so sudden, you wouldn't have noticed
A habit you had, of ignoring any of my protesting actions

Could you ever do right by me?
I think you're incapable of penitence
Nothing stultifies my hope for us
More than your apathetic voice and emotionless touch
I'm leaving this terrible circle of horrors,
Your fun house of puppet shows
Where you can watch me twitch
This way and that, fidgeting awkwardly in your control
I can't live off a mere pittance of your heart
Shriveled, I can't survive off a smidgen of freedom

CHAPTER III : Clenching Fists (Anger)

I'm out, away from venomous toxins at last
I do have more than one thing to offer this world
If you only took the initiative to see, its merit is unmatched
Could you not put in the effort or did you simply not care?
It's too late now; I did leave a legacy all my own
That only fools concentrate on the surface alone

CHAPTER IV

ELEMENTS
(Earth, Wind, Fire, Water)

Women of the Sky

Sky Cotton
Cloud
Pale white
Floats above in her bloated dress
Pregnant
Swollen round breast ready to pour
Rain
Smooth face like porcelain
Translucent eyes and colorless hair
Cotton suspended in air
Puff

Madame Lightning
She flashes her swords
Dress of sparkling light clinging to her hips
None dare kiss her lips

Luminary Sphere
Drenching earth with her scorching smile
Eyes able to burn through darkness
Round full-figured curves
A beauty which melts hearts
Turns eyes into ash
Orb of the daystar

CHAPTER IV : Elements (Earth, Wind, Fire, Water)

Forbidden Underwater Palace

A sweet body of water with angelfish
If you dive deep enough and hold your breath
Its weight will pull you below
Its undertow, so rough
But you love the feeling, irresistible
That something in this world wants you

The water shines without sun
Let it enfold you with tenderness
Force your eyes open
Feel the water pushing against your nature
Denizens of the deep dancing around
Reflective like the beauty of sacred gems
Encasing you in warmth and serenity
This secret city is waiting
Come and rest with us forever
In this waterbed of silky seaweed you can relax
So that we may massage your strained body with mystical oils
And ease your consciousness with the scent of river flowers

Remember, you cannot breathe here
Now is not your time, perhaps in another dream
Do not be so foolish as to ignore the wisdom I share
So desperate to make it through the doors
You would much rather drown in our wet pleasures

And let the liquid into your lungs
Than fight back to the surface
Only to lose sight of this erogenous palace
Saving your life

Do not kill yourself seeking this perfection
And do not reach for what never existed
Or you are bound to drown in your dreams
Just to die in your sleep

CHAPTER IV : Elements (Earth, Wind, Fire, Water)

Life of the Rock
(Traditional Japanese Form, Haiku)

You're hard and filthy
Just sitting your days away
Inanimate rest

E. TARA SCURRY

The Rock's Agony
(Traditional Japanese Form, Haiku)

Resting silently
Until someone steps on you
Then, your cracking scream

CHAPTER IV : Elements (Earth, Wind, Fire, Water)

Master of the Sun

I have your soul on my fingertips
You can only attempt to refuse me
I am the Master of the sun
Never to be diffused

Let your heart fill with water
Your eyes will never savor release
There is no crying in my arena
Harsh tears have no place

Sorrow never hangs
From the eyes of my inhabitants
Ignorant menials crave my blessings
I am encompassing light

No one knows any relief
Let alone my beaming wonder
I am the sole alleviation
You are bequeathed

E. TARA SCURRY

Cloudburst
(Traditional Japanese Form, Haiku)

Like a rush of tears
Landing on my tender cheeks
You fall with power

CHAPTER IV : Elements (Earth, Wind, Fire, Water)

Praise the Rays II
(Traditional Japanese Form, Haiku)

The heated warm rays
Sent to comfort my cold soul
Merciful angels

E. TARA SCURRY

After the Rain
(Traditional Japanese Form, Haiku)

Cool rain falls slowly
The moist air flutters around
Teasing the lean grass

CHAPTER IV : Elements (Earth, Wind, Fire, Water)

Sandy Strip of Peace
(Modified Japanese Form, Haiku)

A beach soft and tan
Waves adorn the moistened sand
We drift asleep on its shore
Pain and trouble are no more

E. TARA SCURRY

Earth

The earth is alive
Her heart is the heated core
Skin, cool soil
Grass, the thin hair of her arms

We are the microorganisms
Sometimes we do right by her
Other times we don't
And she flushes us away in floods
Warps us with disease
Or rips us apart with hurricanes
Her antibiotics
Destroying us all, good and bad

Like bacteria
We've found ways to adapt
To flee and protect ourselves
We sicken her then
Poison her veins with our waste
Gorge ourselves fat with her blood
Like vicious powerful parasites

CHAPTER IV : Elements (Earth, Wind, Fire, Water)

Natural Lullaby

I do not sleep well at night
I have not, for some time
Years
Not since I breathed as a junior in high school
Not since I realized my life
Was in my own hands

If I must sleep for a particularly important occasion
A cup of herbal tea
And rectangular herbal spheres my mouth may take
I will awaken once or twice
Instead of four or five

Other than particularly early occasions
I let my body do as it will
Toss and turn, sleep some, wake some
Reflect on a book I've read or
Fantasize
About my future
I am nocturnal
Preferring to wake and work in the silence of night
Like my balding black cat
With her strange sense of time
Sleeping in the light and the night
At the foot of my bed or
On my papers or stray clothes

I rest best with the electricity off
Window slightly open
To be soothed into sleep by the birds and
Chatting of insects
The creamy white light blinks from my window
I don't mind the light when I sleep
It makes me feel as though I am outside
On a blanket on the grass
Without biting bugs and pulsating rays
But gentle light
And a lukewarm breeze
Rocking me slow like a baby

Beautiful day
Come that I may lay my face against you
Settle in your arms
With no dark shadows to test my nerves
Only your natural lullaby to still
My vibrant thoughts
And meditate on the sound of your breathing
As I lay limp in your arms

Sweet Tempest II

I am the Storm
I fantasize of being gentle as snow
White and innocently weak
Pure and captivatingly feminine
Snow holds the love of many souls
They pray for these tumbling white tears
And dream of snowy jubilees
As their eyes twitch with sleep

Few gaze at my clouds with tenderness
They usually look at me with contempt
Frowning as they reschedule their picnics
Cursing as I ravage their weddings

No one yearns for my embrace
The scared quiver at my voice
And the masses shiver at the touch
Of my winds or the stings of my rain

I throb power and drool rain
Stridently pouring out my heart
Drowning in my own deliriums
Worshiping my own essence
Because there is no one else
To welcome my magnificence

They will sleep in the mires I create
Dwindle in the windy breeze of my luster
With ease they are overcome by the
Fists of my lightning
As they gasp for air in
The heavy dust-filled tears of my clouds

My desire to be valued
Becomes an unfortunate reality to a few
Destitute spirits so addicted to my beauty
Unable to discern the danger within me
Collapse as sinless victims
Smashed lovingly
Into any willing object
Artistically crushed
By my sensual violence

Then I pull myself from my satisfaction
Allowing the clear sky of day to sneak pass me
And carrying as much remorse of
Their death and defeat
As they have love for me

So I sleep easily and with only vague fantasies of guilt
Not meant to be remembered by morning's light

So when my voice whimpers as thunder in
A low and somber tone
Or my eyes flash in the cradle of my lightning
Know that I am not truly unhappy or angry
Because others do not love me

Because I sleep easily and with only vague fantasies of guilt
Not meant to be remembered by morning's light

CHAPTER IV : Elements (Earth, Wind, Fire, Water)

Unnatural Disaster

Woe it was unto the innocent and poor
Gigantic underwater earthquake drowning
Babies, tearing husbands from wives
Brothers and sisters and relatives never to set eyes
On one another until the next life

What a clever idea it was, blame it on Gaia,
Blame it on the Lord
It is man who is not blameless
Using their weapons under the seas,
Killing for their own purpose, hundreds of thousands
In about twelve disparate nations!

What a clever idea it was, blame lack of technology
Lack of monitoring, lack of notification systems
Who has heard of "lack of technology" in this age?
In an area prone to these storms of death of the past
Man didn't want to save lives that day

What a clever idea it was, leveling the pitiable beachfront
Sweeping away the poor, creating sympathy
Making room for the privileged to lay their nests of riches
Yes, so that money pours into the hands of man
Already prepared to receive it, so strategically placed they were
That they may plant their seeds of business without resistance
Under the guise of relief

Let a sociologist write a headline
Let the world step above and look back at itself
Without logs and dust in their eyes
Without their hands tied behind them, on
Their knees worshiping money they don't have
Praying shamelessly for self-interest and pleasure

Man thinks he is clever, but he is foolish
Justice is not ripe and grows on a tree in Eden
The hour it descends, the Son too shall fall from the clouds

Pray for the foolish man
Pray for the innocent and poor
Their souls snatched from the rural shores

CHAPTER V

TEARS OF ANGELS
(Pain and Sorrow)

A Comfort Woman's Testimony

I am sick and heated
The ceiling a blur before me
Yes, the numbness of my body is a blessing
But who is this that gives me mercy?
Since I know no god exists anymore
Because she's left me

She ignores my tears
As they seep into her bosom and disappear with my faith
She does not hold me nor protect me
She does not love me
And every other moment it is a different evil man
With the same full and evil swords
By which they bleed me
And drown my dignity and strength

I weep before they even look at me
I weep before they even beat at my head
I weep when I hear even the faintest sounds
Of their terrible murmurs and laughs

I cannot escape this tragic routine
Look, my legs are numb
They do not move, they cannot run

CHAPTER V : Tears of Angels (Pain and Sorrow)

The doors and windows are guarded
They do not open for me, no light comes through
So here I lie
Hardly alone and hardly alive
My spirit is dead
Yet I survive
Or rather I am merely existing
As the evil man's pleasure
During the evil man's war

Accept the Lies

Drift
The leaves fall
Like my hope

Come
Let's slip off
Float down
The wind can tousle our hair

Jump
There is peace below
Everyone smiles
There are flowers
Which are meant for the dead
Then why do lovers give them?

Don't waste time
Eternity is no more
It was a lie
Like my life
And like our happiness

CHAPTER V : Tears of Angels (Pain and Sorrow)

Algebra is Evil

All this confusion is feeding off my patience
Leave, I don't mind being the only one who sees wild things misplaced
Giving my soul to it, day into the night; still no understanding
Eventually it'll be clear, not like a crystal; like a pencil in water it is not what it seems
But it's taking too long, numbers within themselves, this is ridiculous
Relieve me of this; it has no use to my aspirations; I do not need to know this
Always on my mind, I must pass to continue, such useless madness
Idiot? No, I'm not. I just don't like it. I hate it. Pointless problem solving
Someone get me out of this class; this is the last place I want to be
Enough of this nonsense; letters and numbers don't mix, like water and oil
Violently, let us destroy and break this cycle of evil; I'm through with it
Illuminating the need of its destruction and its obvious evil; let's strike
Lastly, deliver me from its lingering evils, Shepherd. May I never see it again!

Alone

I don't understand this plan
All I know is I'm alone
By myself, empty
With no one to touch my skin
How do I know I'm alive?
No one to hold my hand as I die

CHAPTER V : Tears of Angels (Pain and Sorrow)

Comfort of the Clouds

Love promised by your voice
Yet your heart held no moral,
Forever at quarrel
With your lips
Heart
Broken

The clouds here
They weep with me
Falling now, the rain
Encasing me, embracing me
Comforting
Hug

The Sky Is Really Green

I'm tired of being confused
Of feeling used, playfully abused
Taken for granted
I don't understand it

I'm fed up with being undervalued
I'm sweeter than apples dipped in golden candy
A precious crystal flower, unable to be sold
Let my magnificence be told

I'm sick of guys faking
I just want to see their skin baking
In the heat of my madness and frustration
Let them feel the bloody sting of castration

I'm mad that the joke is true, in numerous cases
That men are just like parking spaces
All the good ones are taken
And the rest are handicap, what a cruel fact

I'm weak with the struggles of emotional health
I wither and fall like a brown dirty leaf
Smeared with grime and flat from being under feet
Into an empty march of circles, the wind bullying me around
Swimming this way and that, without really moving anywhere

CHAPTER V : Tears of Angels (Pain and Sorrow)

I'm dead because none of my needs have been fed
All my time and energy that's been shed
Has peeled off back in the day
When I wasn't nervous and knew what to say
My heart doesn't beat; I expose nothing but defeat

All I know is I'm black, or something like that; and as a matter of fact
The sky is really green, and I'm a pitiful scene
Nothing is real anymore!
Because the world is mean, everyone seems to be fraudulent fiends
With kindness taken for granted, I can't stand it
Anymore, I wish to walk through this door
To a cozy room and bed
Where I can be bled
Of all my suffering chaos; let it shed
So I may, for once, close my eyes
And see light, not darkness
Hope, not loss
But at what cost?
Who can afford happiness
When you're weighed down in the heavy,
Slow, and suffocating poverty
Of your own depression and ill-fated spirit?

Lost To You

As you cry I will not
Touch your eyes
I want to see you truly feel
What it is like to feel
You deserve no comfort
No palm shall rest on your shoulder
No hand shall rub upon your back
Have the strength to embrace
Your errors

Weep will I inside myself
For what may have been
But for you
Your errors
Your terrible, unappreciative, and unaffectionate
Errors
Your negligence

Now you feel; you discern
What you had because it is
At this very instant
Justifiably
Lost to you
Leave will I because I
Love you more than life
Leave will I because I
Love me more than death

CHAPTER V : Tears of Angels (Pain and Sorrow)

Cry now then
I will not soothe your puffy eyes
There is no needle which can mend your errors
There is no tonic which can cure my ache
Nevertheless
Move my muscles do
Love my heart shall
Breathe my lungs will
Skin it does feel
Heart it does heal

E. TARA SCURRY

Not in Love

I fell in love as
Quickly as snowflake would melt
On your skin
Because when I feel your heat,
I'm finished
I melt into you
Can't pull you out of my veins
You're always there
Running through me, burning my heart
Testing the limits of my patience
I overflow from you
I cannot see because of you
Get out of my way

You've only given me a sick ache
Of hopelessness
You, who only drug, party, drink, steal, lie
Liar

My eyes are like terrible and sad holes
Which you've shot through my head with your pistol
They should bleed now, but instead they cry
I want to take your gun out of its shoebox
The same gun which you showed to me with pride
You let me touch it; it was heavy
I want to let my fingers drift along its black barrel now
Perhaps I'll put myself out of this misery

CHAPTER V : Tears of Angels (Pain and Sorrow)

You've put me into
No
You wouldn't even care
No

I'm not in love with you
I just wasn't in love with myself

Numbness of Luxury

I don't want to look back at myself
I will see what I wish not
I will see that I am human
I will see that I have feelings
I will see that I'm alive

I don't want to be here
I don't want to be
I don't want to feel
Take emotion away from me

I want to be numb like steel
I want to be cold like ice floating
On the freezing breaths of the Arctic Ocean
So cold and alone and quiet

That's where I want to be
Where I can be liberated
Away from life's emotion
Floating so happy
So cold and alone and quiet
Like the dead
Floating so happy
So happy
On the freezing breaths of the Arctic Ocean

CHAPTER V : Tears of Angels (Pain and Sorrow)

Sacrilege

How could you look into my eyes, past the tears
And try to make me believe I should forget?
How could you hold my hand, caress my wounds,
And tell me that I must move forward?

You were not present those hours
When they struck me repeatedly
You weren't there
When they broke my boundaries

When I stare back into myself
I can't progress with this life
It's inside me, forbidden to be released
I can't escape me
These cruel memories
Take hold sharply and slice me awake

Just last week, you decided to treat me to breakfast
I sipped my tea in that beautiful restaurant
With the marble tiles and bronze railings
I felt heavy, stiff, and I was tired
You looked at me with arched brows, tilted your head
Almost worried, you implored on my behalf
You noticed water forming at the corners of my eyes
I expressed it was only the steaming tea which irritated
You must have believed me, because you nodded
Commenting upon the tea's potency

Carrying on with your vivacious ways
But I lied, for you had tamed me well
I lied to myself and I lied to you
Because when I lifted the cup to my lips
I gazed down and saw my eyes' reflection
Deep inside they oozed locked nightmares
Denting and breaking their teeth
On bleeding gums to get free of chains
Scratching down their own flesh
To ease violent frustrations

I don't sleep; rest is unknown to me
Peace is a luxury I'm unable to afford
Rip my insides apart so that I may die
I don't want to live
I wish they would have just killed me
And finished the damage they began
I can't live with this

Don't tell me to look past it
Who are you to dictate what's best for me?
I relive my worst nightmare every moment there's silence
You didn't see when I was slapped
You didn't see when I was scratched
And you don't know how it feels
To be the object of sadistic violation
The penetration of terrible things

When it was done, blood dry on my lips
Fingers flinching in the dark, it was cold
My shuddering breath hardly visible
Through my blurred vision and swollen brows
I wanted to cry out for angels' comfort
But my throat was dry and sore with my previous screams

CHAPTER V : Tears of Angels (Pain and Sorrow)

It hurt to cry because of the mutilations across my face
Yet my tears wasted no time mingling with the blood
I drifted into pits of mirrors where I can only look at myself
At this pitiful mess of a fool and victim I've become
I can never be the same; this pain drives over me
Over and over, yet it refuses to crush me to death
Because I have something of strength inside me
Never to breathe freedom and never to be consoled

You don't see me when the lights flicker
How I throw myself into my bed
And cover up with a mass of blankets
As if they could protect me from my own dark shadows

My wrists were strangled and raw
I looked into the heated eyes of my inconsiderate predators
So many, who was who?
Who was it that hit me and who was it that pulled my hair?
Who was it that bruised my shoulders as they tore away my mere coverings?
Was it you, you, or all of you?

Who plunged into my temple
And laughed at my blood?
Someone caressed my insides without a shred of mercy
Then another yelled for me to get up, just to knock me down
They all tainted my temple

I had shivered in a pool of my own agony
I didn't know anything at that moment
My mind was blank, yet somehow full
I hoped my imbroglio would end and relief grow
I simply wanted to die, for them to finish
I thought about what an imbecile I was

I just knew I'd pass on into the next Hell too; it felt near enough
Would I bleed to death or would their rough fingers
Never release their hold on my neck?

My eyes blinked twice and water seemed to pour from them
Silent I grew yet I choked on my own bloody gargle
Finally I stopped physically resisting
Yet my fury never faltered
Staring off into the shadows, I dreamed a lovely dream
That someone emerged and slit my throat, ending my turmoil
It was all so blurry, but my mind was alive!
And I had stopped kicking long ago
Just enough for me to swallow the blood mess in my throat

But you weren't there; you never were there when needed
How can I ever marry the man of my dreams when I have nothing anymore?
My worth was stripped away like skin
And shreds of my dignity blew in the wind of my grief

I am nothing but a shriveled rose, void of color and vibrancy
Tossed out and disregarded, because I wasn't desirable anymore

You ordered me to forget, but was it really best for me?
I was destroyed long ago when I was desecrated piece by piece
Under the beauty of the moon and in the arms of the night's heat

How can anyone love me now?
No one will love a tortured soul
Who has the stomach to touch a lacerated body?
No one wants a tortured girl on the brink of insanity

Excruciating hopelessness is an accessory I wear around my neck
I'm that outsider, sitting alone on the park bench
So friendly and quietly pleasant if approached

CHAPTER V : Tears of Angels (Pain and Sorrow)

And then something lights my fire, sparks
Tears submerge my battered cheeks and people wrap their arms around me
I can never spill the agonies of my traumatization for anyone
Words have no place in the story of my experience
The nightmare, an inexplicable Hell upon earth
It's one of those recurring dark reveries, but it's real
It won't leave me alone!
I tried to do what you said, attempting to pray it all away
It's there, I admitted it to myself, why can't you?
Why did you tell me that no one would believe me?

Look at me!
Look into my eyes, deeply
Just dare to take a look!
No? Because you know it's true!
If you can't even look at me, how do you expect me to look at myself?
I don't understand you, I hate you!

Something happened to me; it's a story I'm able to tell
I was walking in the park, trying to think of pleasant things
And this lady in a full old-fashioned dress caught my gaze
I had never seen this lady before, but she came to me
I don't know why, but I didn't move
She took my hands in hers and shook her head slowly
Without warning, I started to cry
I never knew her name or why she looked at me that way
But she saw into me; I must have been clear as glass
I had fallen to my knees and onto the grass; I cracked
My rain sank into her long dress; I clutched the hem tightly in my hands
Her plump fingers went about my head soothing me
Then I slipped onto the grass and tumbled from her

The flowers seemed to soothe my eyes and wipe my tears
And then, I awoke in my room
I didn't know what happened or how it ended
But my knees itched; they were grass-stained

Days pass as they normally do and I think about that lady
Her short brown hair and soft eyes
Those full plump arms of hers that I could throw myself into
She looked as through I could tell her of my demons, my atrocity
I just wanted to live in her embrace, someone to rub my back
To let me know everything is all right
That it wasn't my fault and I wasn't to blame
Though I feel it was, just for being me

I used to hold my head up and I knew I could do anything
But I was bashed down; I'll never be the same

There was a violation in the tabernacle of my body
This sadness is a part of me, as I'm a part of it
A house, but not a home
No one will take me in, because I can not let it out

CHAPTER V : Tears of Angels (Pain and Sorrow)

Screwed Over In The Dark

Floating on the boat of despair
The river of tears sending me forth
Eyes stinging from cold fear

Will you always be there for me
Or did you speak false seduction
For your own wicked amusement?

So that I may lie trusting beside you
Heart and body naked before those eyes
For you to break and take at your will

I'm sad and surprised
I thought you really loved me
Then why did you hold me,
Look deep into my eyes, and tell me lies?

I have passion in my pain
All this love-wishing was in vain
I don't want to spend a lifetime looking for someone
But you just had me, then left
For more fun

I have no love, no hope left, and no heart
You left it bleeding,
Still beating in the dark

Sad Faces

I walk these streets
Inevitably, I look around and I see sad faces
Children and adults
Pushed along by grim reapers
Sharp staffs in their backs

I move along quietly, realizing my helplessness
Because the screams of their eyes deafen me
Into a vicious fever of pity I can't express

CHAPTER V : Tears of Angels (Pain and Sorrow)

The Light and Blades

Where was my sun
When I opened my eyes
Where was my blanket
When I was freezing in the tomb of misery
A little black cherry blossom
Run over by brutal blades
Do you know how that feels
to have metal tearing into you?

But you never saw the light
Because you were the light
And blinded by your own brightness,
You never saw me
You never protected me
You never loved me

Scattered
Along the sandy ocean
With no true soil to plant my roots
Where is the rest of myself
It was run over by the brutal blades
Me, the little black cherry blossom
Do you know how that feels,
to have metal tearing into you
and never die,
to have your insides clawed out
and not be able to cry?

To the Light I Stumble

I am searching for me
Deeper and deeper
Dark and dreary
Cannot see my own
Hands in front of me
Bang
Bang
Run

Follow the voice
Follow the aching agony
Follow the path that hurts,
Blood-smeared rocks underfoot
Broken twigs

To the light I stumble
To this cliff I crumble, down
Landing
Thud
Encompassing pain
I am not found
Though there is light
Ahead

CHAPTER V : Tears of Angels (Pain and Sorrow)

Trickling Out Over the Lovely Violets

Dream of your precious peace
Wake up weeping over
Promises never meant to be kept
Eternal, peace has no meaning
Mix our blood
Lay me in silence

Death
In a tomb unmarked
dreams of peace, worthless dreams
Gash away my throat
No need to speak of such miserable agony
Unable to be expressed through the
Frail and weak words of man
Trickling out in thick disgusting globs
Here over the violets
Such lovely violets ...

Breathing my last breath
To the songs of beautiful bluebirds
Cheek pressed upon shades of infantile purple
Living in the hope of dreams
Dying in the hope of dreams

Bloody White Roses

The cup is half full, she yearns for more
He chokes his feelings while choking her
Suffocating their vows
Crucifying his love for her
While everyone can see it up there
Beautiful and bleeding
For her eyes to gaze upon it
Glorious and needing
Will he ever share with her why?
Why are closed wounds still bleeding?

Raining onto her white flowers
Staining them with traumatized baggage
Don't stain her flowers with crimson
Any marriage staggers when nurtured by blood
Which oozed from a dark and high cloud
Hardly able to see him up there
Leaving her so far from the truth
Raining on her, drowning her, and confusing her
Leaving her inebriated with his grief
Dragging her down in his luscious gravity

CHAPTER V : Tears of Angels (Pain and Sorrow)

Caressing her against his baggage
It trickled from above, alive in her hair
Down to bruised cheeks, stinging her eyes
Seeping into her clothes
Exposing beaten love for him to see
Permanently staining her skin with his fate
She cries when he pushes her away
She doesn't understand why
Yet as she drifts away in his rain
She remembers he'll always love her
As his palm strikes her face

With Death Comes Peace

I believe in tears
I believe in fate
So many things in the world I hate
But I can't shake off
My own shadow

I lust for success,
For my eyes to sparkle against bright riches
And for my heart to be overflowing from love

Yet someone is trying to shove me off this steep slope
And I'm too weak to resist

I'm void
I believe in the death of hope
I wish I could believe in equal mutual love
Where one day I may be content
I must find the perfect erotic masculine fruit
But the trees have deteriorated and fallen
The handsome harvest plucked at their ripe peak
As always, there is nothing left for me

At the moment, my soul is distorted with urge
Acknowledging this, I requested to tan in the rays of peace
But my peers and the society ignored me
So I lay, hollow and quiet

CHAPTER V : Tears of Angels (Pain and Sorrow)

They watch me drain casually,
like the precious tears from my eyes
They are helpless against it, as I am
But you soothe my welts
By loving me in any method I allow
Because soon it will be over in one last gentle breath
I will collapse comparable to those barren and deteriorated trees
And I'll fall like a waterfall of weakness
Smashing into smooth rocks,
breaking my neck against the pebbles of longing
At that moment, I may discover the answer to my woes
And with my death, peace may arise
And only then perhaps, I may sip of freedom

Double Bind

Clotho, Lachesis, and Atropus, weave now
Let your needles prick at my skin if they must
Teeth are gnawing away all my lingering strength,
The sweet dissolution of hope

Little shovels digging upward
The soft hair on my flesh
Roughly scooping the cells already dead
Divulging the monster deep within me

The Moerae, proceed
Spin that terrible fate here before me
I can do nothing
But remain sane and unmoved

Every time I am pushed
And my boundaries crucified
It is a multitude of throbbing wounds
Necessities I can't live without

My limbs are slow and weak
This mouth of mine dry with complaint
All I see as I struggle to lift my eyes
Is a glass of hemlock with dashes of arsenic

As such it is the way it must be
It is also the end
It is a powerful slap
That awakens my world

CHAPTER V : Tears of Angels (Pain and Sorrow)

Ich Werde Immer Bei Dir Sein
(I'LL ALWAYS BE WITH YOU)

Into a little box
A sharp glass box
I look in
You hang, rope on throat, chained and hardly alive
All around you I am here
Keeping you dumb and supple to my use
User, abuser
I am he

See you standing naked inside
Inside my sharp little glass box
Trapped, hands sticking to the walls
Ashamed and helpless
Cry because I will it
Slice your flesh in frustration
It feels good to you, that release
Everyone can see you inside
My sharp little glass box

Tears in your flesh
Shiny sweet razor blade
Blood swells
Drips down your creamy arms
Released from pain, only for an instant

You are still inside my sharp
Little glass box—naked, shallow breaths
Stifled

Everyone can see you, dumb and supple to my use
Razor wounds decorating your arms
Painful bracelets, so beautiful to me
I let you bleed yourself weak
Every time
May you remain such, so drained of strength
That you cannot lift a voice, a foot, a will
To break my sharp little glass box

I am your master, your lover
But I don't love you
I say I do, but I don't
I am in love with the power, the control
Not you
You are the weakest, most pathetic thing I know
I love the way you make me feel; you're addicted to me
And I to you
You're too stupid to realize why
Too pathetic to act on what you know you should do
Scream for me! I can always hear how in control I am
Cry for me, bleed for me
Mutilate on the outside
The inside
Is taken care of

Smack you, dumb fool
Stay in line, under my heavy heel
Bleed yourself weak and low self-esteem
Everybody can you see; you're embarrassed
I hold you in the palm of my will

CHAPTER V : Tears of Angels (Pain and Sorrow)

Onto your lips rest my stones
Into your belly, weighted low self-esteem
Ich werde immer bei dir sein

I've twisted you painfully tight, around me
When away, all over your thoughts
Sometimes your bruised flesh
All over your arms you look there
And remember why
Me
Unlike *you*, I don't use razors
Slit your throat with my threats
No one will hear you, my love
You can't tell
Much less scream
I know you're afraid of being alone
Without me
Alleine (Alone)
I do what I want

I'm in control; it just tickles me silly to see you
Try to scream, empty voice, empty veins
Every day another ounce drips away
Into my ego
My daily amusement, dumb fool
You don't have feelings; you're crazy
Mental
Just look at what you do to yourself
At what you let me do to you
I can't really hurt you; you don't deserve to be
Treated like a woman
You're dying and gnawing at your own flesh
Like a dumb and desperate animal gnawing off its foot
That's caught in a stinking spiked trap

My only fear is that you actually realize I'm not the one
For you, even though you are the one for me

I have as much sympathy for you as
This dead baked piece of chicken on my plate
Killed and dead for my use
Parsley for pretty, good to cut into pieces
Supple meat, good to eat

You're just roasting now, baby
Roasting alive, the smoke of your flesh
Smelling of helplessness
Powerlessness
And I love it!
How bad is it going to get before you leave me?
It's a waiting game
I'm hungry and you're losing
I know you're afraid of being
Alleine

I've twisted you painfully tight, around me
You need my heat, even though it burns
Every time, every time, but you keep touching, baby
You never learn
All I have to say is sorry
And you jump back into my simmering pot
Until it boils over again
You know what the definition of *insane* is?
Doing the same thing over and over again
And expecting a different result, bitch

I like you, stupid, dumb fool
Stay with me at my side in my
Sharp glass box, boiling pot

CHAPTER V : Tears of Angels (Pain and Sorrow)

And simmer and evaporate away
Your dreams and self-esteem, respect
Until there's nothing but a disgusting sticky mess
A pathetic, old, and stinking ugly blob
Under my feet
That I have to scrape against the sidewalk to get rid of
And I will
Every last bit of you, for someone else
When I finally tire of your stupidity and you're
No longer fun to misuse

I never really wanted you anyway
Just loved the way you made me feel
Powerful and in control, needed
Every time you said sorry when you did
Nothing wrong, except
Remain anchored to me
Like a blind man to his dog except
I don't care where I'm taking you
Or like
A priest to his Bible when he's burning at the stake
Everyone around begging for him to forsake God
But to no avail, and yes I am your god
You'll burn and bleed before leaving me
I don't worry; I save that for you
Because I know for a fact
You can't get away from me
Ich werde immer bei dir sein

Void of Essence

You're drawing the life out of me
I'm collapsing into myself
Yet distress doesn't invade me
And I lay lacking verve

I am empty like the clouds
After a spiteful rain
Without a rainbow
Or the honey of the sun

CHAPTER VI

WHITE HOLE
(Miscellaneous)

Slipping

Relax, love, and hold hands with truth
Times are hard and so am I
Tell me what troubles you
I am not all knowing
Your eyes speak in sad colors
Draw a parasite portrait with a crayon called depression
None are surprised; this weary sorrow crumbling
Down your cliff to nowhere
As always, never ending as the stars
That beat down bright and blinding against your dreams

I see you flickering away in your own darkness,
Slow and sure
Hardly the exuberant candle that you were
That light of yours, fading into emptiness
Your hopes and dreams blessed in ashes
Going down forever, it would not be wise to do this together
I don't want to come down with you
Into your pitiful little pit of shame
I cannot help you stop the suffocating hands
Clawing you down, naked and bruised

I grow agitated when you stare at me
Every day your pain plucks another feather of love
And happiness from your eyes
So cold, suicidal, and serene they are
Yet you continue to laugh and force a grin

CHAPTER VI : White Hole (Miscellaneous)

It only conceals the wounds from everyone but yourself
This is why I know the Devil's telling you jokes again
Why warm yourself with heated blankets of Hell's agony?
You seem to exist only for the prospect of Hell's fire
Walking and swimming in a pool of anguish you yourself nurtured
His arms caress you so close; I know you forget to hold your breath
He soothes you so softly that you usually forget these important things
Lies easing their way past his dark full lips
Seducing you as perfume and candy to the child-man you are

You're already falling, stepped off the cliff a long time ago
Why not snatch onto a branch along the side
And hold on for whatever dear life you have left?
Don't abandon your grip; I know those fingers bleed
Just hold tight, climb up and push yourself upward
Kick against the claws dragging you low and miserable
Sever the insults and guilt weighing you down
Or even cling with all your strength
As your feet dangle against the air
Abiding in the veins of lonely despair
Enduring the brisk ache of gravity
Lift yourself to painful vitality

Clear The Way

My heart drags on a barbed wire
As the stories of saints are realized
I recall a memory
I fantasized smashing the pudgy pigeons
Who gathered begging at my feet as I
Sprinkled bread
Fearless
They only felt hunger
While my dangerous feet were
Ignored

How fearless they were
How their hunger overrode any horror
I could not hurt them
So then
How could they hurt my saints?
Soaked with the Rain of Hope
Their pain of toil, precious saints
Scorch their lights onto my face

I see my dream coming true
As I lie, gazing into the sky now
Up and through breaking glass
Shatter like a terrible rain
The Rain, I have questioned
Glass into my skin
The blood of only those

CHAPTER VI : White Hole (Miscellaneous)

Saints
Who can give birth
They crucified saints who
Pushed the nails into their own
Breast
To bleed for me

Punched through the glass with
Delicate naked hands
To make way for me
That I may follow without terrible wounds
Relief is here, yet the goal still lies in fragments
The Rain of Hope persists
The pain of the glass
Is a terribly sweet agony
Let it cut me
I still go through
No longer outside watching
But inside, clear of the storm

I penetrate through the ceiling
I hold the delicate bleeding hands of
These saints, our blood mingles
We are sisters in this struggle

The Circle

More meat means more meat to sell
Stuff the animals with growth hormones
Like brown stuffing in a dead turkey
Bloated, juice dripping down the side

I eat them animals and get fat
I eat them animals and get sick
Maybe I'll staple my stomach
Maybe I'll eat less
Okay, I ate less, but I'm still fat because
I'm still eating growth hormones
No one wins except them meat and diet industries

Meatier cows means more meat to sell
A fatter me means I eat more
So I buy me more meat
I might buy a gym membership
I buy more diet food, I have more hospital bills
Since I eat meat, I'm much more likely to get
Breast, colon, and prostate cancer, arthritis, stroke
High blood pressure and veins in my legs
My chances of getting that are higher than those
Strange vegetarian folks
Eating their funny food, drinking their 100% juice and anti-milk
They must know something I don't, to deprive themselves of real food
Kinda like them religious folks, trying to be perfect

CHAPTER VI : White Hole (Miscellaneous)

Maybe they know something I don't, to deprive themselves of the good life

I know that some farmers put in tranquilizers
To keep the animals calm, but I don't mind that
I eat the meat and tranquilizers be good for my own nerves
They put antibiotics in them too, that's good for me
I get free medicine every time I eat me some chicken or steak
So what if it makes me more resistant to penicillin
If I already have free medicine, I don't need penicillin

Over a lifetime, we eat about 750 chickens and turkeys
About thirty-six pigs
Meat got protein, lots of protein
They say it takes more energy to digest meat than we get from eating it
That our digestive organs wear down because of it, causing all sorts of stuff
Meat has a lot of fat, but I like my meat and milk
A car cost less than a hamburger, per pound
Eating meat might not be good for the planet, because of the industry
It messes up the water, air, and soil and takes ten times more energy than
It takes to satisfy them vegetarian eaters
If everybody like me reduced animal eating by 10%
The hungry of the world could be fed, because of the grain saved

It's not the nicest thing to do, to overcrowd animals in the stockyards
But I don't see it, so it's all right with me
It's not like they're *real* animals, like cats, dogs, horses, and bunnies
Those are nice, friendly animals
Chickens, cows, and hogs don't count

I don't see baby cows chained to dark pens so small they can't sit
Taken at birth to be slaughtered as veal, never to see light
I don't see live animals dangling from the ceilings, blood swelling their faces
I don't see castration with scorching heat
With no pain relief, so they don't mate

It's cheap to stick a long rod through their anus to their mouth until they die or
Stun them with electricity, slitting their throats to preserve the carcass
Decapitation, scorching and drowning them alive in boiling water to
Soften their skin for picking feathers and tender meat
I know it happens, it's true, but I don't see it so it's all right
Many times them chickens are starving and anxious, they try to eat or peck each other
So their beaks are seared off without anesthesia
Chickens should know better than to pick at each other like that

Slaughterhouses violate more laws than any other type of business
Not just in the treatment but in the chemicals they inject
Raw meat covered in goo and blood, nasty
But once it's cooked with a little parsley on the side, it's delicious
I don't want to think about what it really is, who does?
Why do 30% of pigs die of heart attacks before being sliced open?
Maybe they understand the cries of those before them on the butcher line
Maybe they're literally scared to death
But they aren't *real* animals
They don't have feelings and personalities like cats and dogs

Me and everyone else grew up on meat and I won't let it go
So don't try, don't waste your time

CHAPTER VI : White Hole (Miscellaneous)

I don't want fake soy meat, tofu, or imitation meatloaf
I've never had it before, but I'm sure it's awful
The meat I eat isn't gross; it's delicious and juicy
I love the taste of dead castrated animal injected with chemicals
I can't pronounce

Cows and chickens are anxious, depressed, and scared
They breathe the aroma of torture and feel death inevitable
In the dirty dark stench, under the vile shadows of their pens
They produce anxious, depressed, and scared chemicals inside
I eat their anxious, depressed, and scared flesh
And now I must take more calm or happy pills
I'm not ignorant of why I am anxious and depressed
I know that causes it, but that's what my pills are for

I butcher and slice up billions of innocent, feeling animals
So what if it comes back to me; I get killed prematurely too
Breast, colon, and prostate cancer, arthritis, stroke
High blood pressure, heart disease
It's the circle of life
It's the circle of death
That's the way it is and I'm going to eat my meat
I'm going to pollute my earth
I'm going to eat more so the other half of the world starves
God didn't create animals as precious beings
God gave me permission to eat them
Otherwise He wouldn't have made them out of meat (But am
I meat? Doesn't count!)
So what if eating them means they get abused in the process
It's my right and I can't do anything about it
Nothing I want to do
When He said I have dominion over them, He meant
I can torture, impale, electrocute, beat, and break their bones
And mutilate their little squealing bodies

As it pleases me to do so that I may eat and grow fat
That was His purpose; I'm just being obedient

I'm too weak to stop eating meat; I like it
It tastes good
That organic milk is made by hand-milked and grain-eating cows
But the regular milk is made by machine-milked and
Dead-ground-up-cow-eating cows
Machine milking causes irritation, pus and blood get mixed into the milk
I don't know what it would taste like without it, so I can't
Tell the difference, especially with the flavoring chemicals to mask
it, so what
Your nipples would probably get sore, bleed, and ooze pus if
You had a metal machine milking at them for twenty hours nonstop too
That's why it stinks so bad when it gets a little old
And soy anti-milk lasts like five plus times as long in the fridge

Don't matter
I have dominion over women, children, and all animals of the earth
It's fair and it is my divine right
And I'm going to suffer
Just like the animals do when they die
It's the circle
I hurt them and they hurt me
I torture, murder, and castrate them and they
make me fat and give me heart disease!
It's the circle
It's fair

And in our separate ways
We're both too weak to stop it

CHAPTER VI : White Hole (Miscellaneous)

Elevator

I once dreamed I was in a stuffy, crowded elevator
Naked
Sometimes my flesh froze
Sometimes my flesh burned
Always thirsty, hungry, and unable to turn around or sit
Too many people around me, pressed tightly against me
I stood in my own disgusting waste, my feet soaking
I stood in the squishy dark waste of those around me
Stood, for days and nights
I wanted to sit, even in the waste, but there was no room
It stunk, my eyes closed but the stench would not let me sleep
Thirsty, hungry, and unable to turn around or sit

We were enclosed, but I heard through the metal
Crying
Wailing
Death was here, outside this door
We were nervous
Some of us spoke to each other with hoarse voices
About how it was, running free in green pastures
The fresh air, food, and cool drink beside the quiet waters
Days and nights pass
Yelling now, in angry and frustrated dry voices
Others simply cried or beat at themselves
Someone began to eat at my shoulder
I pushed him away but there was nowhere to push

I screamed and bled
My feet stained brown and wet
Someone behind me had been dead for days
Her flesh still stood, supported limply by the surrounding bodies
So pressed together, so awfully pressed

The elevator opened and closed
Three dirty bodies left us, room to move
A woman in the corner took two steps, then back, repeatedly
Two steps then back, two steps then back, like she was crazy

My shoulder was infected, rotting
It stunk and hurt
My feet stained brown and wet
The air rancid
I heard crying, wailing

The elevator opened and closed
I, another man, and the woman who had gone mad were pulled
out
By our hair or ankles, I don't remember
A rough Giant with a snout and tail grabbed a dirty body
I saw the skinny flesh fight weakly and cry out
As the Giant held it down and forced
A long metal rod up his anus
Another smaller rod was inserted between his teeth
The body stiffened as it was electrocuted
Tossed to the side in a heap
In a tall sad pile of twisted limbs and flesh like the Holocaust

The next body in front of me grabbed at her heart
And collapsed to the floor
I prayed my own heart would give way
That I wouldn't have to feel this

CHAPTER VI : White Hole (Miscellaneous)

They began to peel her flesh away
Thank the precious Lord
He let her heart give out, or I would be hearing her terrible screams
As they skinned her alive
Or would it be so painful she could only open her mouth and
Stiffen her wide eyes, lips, and limbs with suffering inexpressible?

I had thick manly hair on my chest
On my back and my legs
The Giant tossed me like a rag doll
Into a large boiling metal cylinder
I felt my flesh melt off its bones
I hoped to drown quickly and gulped water
But it burned my throat away before
It could reach my lungs

Evil Giants, am I in Hell?
What did I do wrong?
Who did I make so angry,
To be so cruel to me?
Where is my God?
Where is my God ... ?
There He is, holding me now
His precious creature, a son of Adam
He loves me
He pets me
What do I need flesh for?
He comforts my tormented spirit
There is no more flesh for the Giants to abuse
He comforts me, feeds me
I stay in sight of his staff; no harm will befall me near it
But I roam free in the green pastures in light, walking upright
I fear no evil Giants with snouts, beaks, and tails, others with black and white spots

I am led beside the quiet waters and drink my fill, never thirsty
I am home, in his house forever
I feel his love
He loves me
He pets me
What do I need flesh for?
He comforts my spirit
What do they need flesh for?
Why do they need flesh?

CHAPTER VI : White Hole (Miscellaneous)

Destination

The road is more dangerous than the sky
You think my head is in the clouds

I am more grounded than you
We both are more likely to die
In a car than in a plane
Does that make planes safer?
No, I don't think so
However, I am more likely to reach my destination
Without getting lost

Cream Of The Crop

All the smart companies who aren't
Afraid
To be the best come
To see you
Most prestigious HBCUs
Whose beds rest the heads
Of the cream of the crop
Young, black movers, shakers
Best investments
Hardly affirmative action
Token coins
But flower beds of diamonds
And golden-brown gems
From the tear showers of their ancestors
Who made exceptional the norm
And average a failure
"*To be on time is late*
to be early is on time
to be late is unacceptable"

Companies who aren't
Afraid
To be the best
Know where the treasure chest lies
Not afraid of these thriving gems
Other companies know what they want

CHAPTER VI : White Hole (Miscellaneous)

And go elsewhere to lose
They know where to avoid
Golden-brown gems
They really only want a good Negro
Not an uppity Negro
Because you can't tell those uppity Negros anything
"*A great man knows his limits*
A wise man knows he has none"

Other schools graduate smart black folks
Who work hard
But these Ivy Leagues of the Black Realm
Graduate geniuses
Golden-brown diamonds
Onyx gems
Who work smart
Smart smart smart
Who will reach peaks
Even you haven't seen
These geniuses don't have a problem with how
You
Wear your natural hair to work
Wash and wear silky straight, wavy or spiked with gel
Why do you have a problem with how
They
Wear their natural hair to work?
Wash and wear tightly curled, thick, coiled or braided
Don't tell them their dreads aren't professional
Or that their hair is too big (they hear and you mean "too black")
When you discriminate, you lose more money than they do
Do you care about that bottom line or
Pleasing the foolish ignorant at your organization?

E. TARA SCURRY

The smart company who isn't
Afraid
To be the best will be the best
Because they know where the flower beds of diamonds and gold lie
Under the blue-and-white sky
Inside maroon and white brick buildings

CHAPTER VI : White Hole (Miscellaneous)

Crackhead

Natural
Can you say you have
Tasted pure air
Or have even felt your true hair?

The subculture of us who are naturally inclined
Want to free your mind
Bring you back to your beauty most divine

I was once an addict; I feel you
I understand you, but I am free and want you to be

You are literally a crackhead, my dear
Addicted to crack, the creamy white kind
Shame on them who make you believe
You are only beautiful chemically altered

Every week of six
Run to the hairdresser to get your fix
Of creamy white crack

Oh have mercy!
If an inch of natural curls
Do doth show!

You will burn and press it into
Submission

Why tame beautiful thick hair?
Is it not better to be free?

Fine then, insecure sister
Forever be a slave
Forever reject the beautiful hair
God
Planted on you
Do you think he would give you ugly hair?
Who then, insecure sister
Are you trying to please?
I know it's not the one you speak to on your knees

Your hair is high
Chemically altered to its detriment
Burned and broken
Crispy fried
And you think it's better this way
Deep down you know, you know
It's not better
You see the damage done when chained with weave
Or chemically overdosed
But it is less threatening
To them
To have you burned and broken in
Forever tamed and never free
Like good little Negros
You see it brittle and falling off your head
With your wisdom

But I mistake
I separate your hair from who you really are
Your hair is high, not you
When your hair is having a bad day
You feel just fine

CHAPTER VI : White Hole (Miscellaneous)

Dangerous Baby Girl

You torture me, baby girl
Come closer, so precious
Would you like some sweets
For my sweet, precious baby girl?
You know I'm wrong
And dangerous
But so are you

Your mother dresses you in hot pants
That short skirt
I see your creamy small legs
So young and soft
Unmarred so far
Flat-chested and tiny all over
You torture me, baby girl
Your mother dresses you in tiny tank tops
Baby flip-flops
Pink skirt; I see your tummy

I've got to have your everything
Stay sweet and silent
Like a baby blueberry in a bush
Picked and squeezed of your innocence
Drenching my fingers in your sweetness
All over my hand

E. TARA SCURRY

I see you looking at me
You love my attention
Your mother always lets me in
Let me buy you dolls and things
Beautiful, why would I lie?
So exposed and innocently sparsely clothed
You torture me
In your flower print tiny shorts
A single strap hanging from your shoulder
Hardly nine years old
You're dangerous, baby girl

Your mommy told you about men like me
You know it's not right
But she dressed you in hot pants
And you love my attention

You drew the cutest picture the other day
I was in your house
Your own father disregarded it
Your mommy hung it up on the fridge
But I told you it was marvelous!
What a talented Picasso you are!
Who's Picasso? The best and most creative artist
Who has ever lived!
And you, my sweet
You are the best I've ever seen!
I know you liked that,
Didn't you
You ate it up and kissed my cheek
You hate to see me go
And I'll keep it that way

CHAPTER VI : White Hole (Miscellaneous)

I'll hurt you a little bit
But it's not my intention
But just indulge me for a few minutes
A few long heated minutes
You're so beautiful, the most precious thing
I've ever seen
In your dangerous hot pants
And pink thin tank top
Your mommy must dress you up like that
Just for me

A Geisha's Death in Winter

I cry and I die
In the arms of the night
The trees are naked and bare

The clouds come down and seem to cradle me
Fog, I cannot see

Salty ice frozen under my eyes
I grow quite numb and beautifully blue

Someone's stabbing me
It hurts, I leak
Yet I'm still and remain unmoved

My senses falter like thin veils in the wind
The snow suckles down my blood

I can recall cherry blossoms falling like rain
The beauty of the memory dulls my pain

No matter how far, I cannot hide
Something is deep inside me

CHAPTER VI : White Hole (Miscellaneous)

Unable to even shiver
I wish for warmth
Yet the moon lacks in offerings or mercy

I had run through this forest
But the thorns bled me
I sank into the icy flowers

It was a man who grabbed me
Dragged by my hair
He sprawled me along the snow

With the taste of amakuchi
Still heavy on my tongue
I was comforted that it had not abandoned me

The blood splattered against my kimono
Which made the birds within the fabric
Seem like they were bleeding

I begin to feel nothing
My skin hard and pale
I pray that I'll finally slip away

Blood Night

Behold its
Life-giving power
Overflowing in one's flesh
Oppressed into veins
Dark and rich

Never go out alone
Intercept with caution
Gangsters, insects, and vampires all
Heated with desire for your blood
Tonight is not your lucky day

Naked Dance

Warped
Into mysteries blue light green
Flashing lights it's all mine
At least for these dear moments
Let's gets stripped and naked
Bare flesh
Bloody bones bouncing heads
Reveal yourself completely open and free
Just for me

Why is it so painful?
Wind scratches your naked skin
Cold bites it
Sun strikes it
Reveal yourself
See your flesh, everything bare
Let it hurt
At least for these sacred moments
Reveal yourself

Dance
Without clothes, move easier
Without fear, close your eyes
Be
Not what you see
Fluttering fingers, waving hands
Sporadic blue light white

Like bolts of lightning
Shocking us out of death
Like a zombie on a cold table
Into life, alive
Into life, alive!

CHAPTER VI : White Hole (Miscellaneous)

Epicurean of the Land

All the prince's brawl without shame
Roses and gems weep at my beauty
Lords and their knights die for me when the moon wakes
Liquor is my voice, creating drunkards of my unwitting sweethearts
Squires and gentlemen collapse at my stimulus
For I am the mistress of power
I am the messiah of pleasure
You'll only dream of kissing my feet
And touching my garments
My body steams from the heat of my endurance
And you'll go mad with insatiable desire
Because I am the queen of myself
I am the queen of you
I am the queen of anyone who breathes of my perfume

Clovers

The clovers, they march into the fog
Little feet light on the green grass
And the lightning comes, the blood
To pieces the clovers splatter
Green gook glowing,
Splashed brutally over the grass

Blood tears of green,
Emerald eyes
Loud squealing cries
Nails of shiny jade
Lime-colored feet
Splattered

Come now, clovers
So soft your bodies
So fresh your scared scent
I know why Ireland loves you
Beware the lightning, my little loves

Into the grave now, little clovers
Cannot tell one body from another
Splattered green goop,
So fragile you are, little clovers
So soft and lovely you are, little clovers
I want to put you out of your misery

CHAPTER VI : White Hole (Miscellaneous)

>Here you all lie, broken and bleeding
>Fresh green olive blood drying on your petals
>Still twitching, poor little clovers
>Squeals weakening into terrible gargling whimpers
>You are not so lucky

Lavender

Lavender is my favorite color
Lavender like lilacs
Lavender like the flowers that cover my green garden
Smooth and silky petals
I like the velvety shade of lavender as the sun sets
Falling asleep in a rainbow at my windowsill
A baby purple, faint, shallow, and never deep; an immature violet
Looking as good as you smell
Feathery, warm, peaceful
Lavender …

CHAPTER VI : White Hole (Miscellaneous)

Time Alone

I have time for myself
Time alone
By myself
To do as I please
I have time on my own
Time for me
All alone
To do whatever I need
It's my favorite time
Time of the day
Or time of the night
When I can do just as I please
Some of my favorite things
Things I enjoy

Do as I want
On my own, all quiet
Or loud
My favorite sounds
When I'm alone
By myself
To do as I please

How Good You Were

I heard about you
Back when Reznor sang of your sweetness
Continuously curious about you
The world let not your name past their lips as I sat
In my health class or as I listened to my elders
All ignorant or dismissive of you
Let the opportunity reveal itself
And I will seek to know you

You took me one evening
I felt your truth, held my blood in your hug
Party time, at the University of Maryland
Mixed and multicultural
It was a typical party, save for your presence

How many years since I first heard your name?
I asked you to take me; how good you were to comply

A traditional ritual in your honor
The infant snowy cube resting gently on a silver bed
Suspended like a hammock over an eager glass
Pouring freezing water over the sugary block,
Crumbling without a fight into your embrace
I gazed into your smoky green eyes

CHAPTER VI : White Hole (Miscellaneous)

They are afraid because they are ignorant
Rumors ran wild, you've been unfairly stereotyped
But I've known you and let the opportunity reveal itself again
I would dip my body into your enticingly warm and soothing tub
Rest my aching shoulders on your rim, let my hair
Rest on your yielding pillow, surrounded by the most
Soothing herbal aroma of star anise, lemon balm, and juniper

I could also refuse you, but why?
I asked you to take me; how good you were to comply

E. TARA SCURRY

Happy Moments

I'm happiest when I'm rushing down a mountain
With my impressive apparel, floating on a blue board
Even as my noggin knocked against metal
Going down smiling, happy as ever on that board
Concussion or no concussion, I was pursuing my dream
Premier black female professional snowboarder, with skills unseen!
Flying me away in a helicopter, away from my
Precious snowy mountain

I'm happiest when I'm in black
Laced up, thick-heeled boots, waving my hands
Gorgeous gothic getup
At a Rammstein concert where they get to finish their set
No matter how little of their bodies lay encased in meager white socks
Passionately enjoying myself, a floating man's boot strikes my skull!
Concussion, concussion; fainting with that bright smile and waving arms
Scooped away in the arms of a guard, away from my
Dear concert

I'm happiest when my face is painted black-and-white
Hanging with my best friend, trying to act crazy like the clowns
Leaving soaked with faygo, sticky with glee and people questioning me
Why do you like them? Aren't they kind of strange and out-there?
Yes, good beats and humor; I appreciate that kind of creativity

CHAPTER VI : White Hole (Miscellaneous)

I'm happiest snuggled on top of a couch with warm sheets and my cat at my feet
With a cup of green tea, white tea, or hot vanilla soymilk swirled
With white mocha hot chocolate on a table near me
Oreos or milk chocolate must be within hand's reach
A book in my palm or a pen between my fingers
I like to draw a little bit, I like to scrapbook a little bit
I love to leave a legacy

Let the Earth Love Me II

Turn the lights out
Time to go to sleep
Waiting
For release
Open my throat and
Expand my lungs
Trying to survive
To breathe

I walk ten times as slow as
The world is busy and festers around me
Bugs of life bite me, scratch, itch, and burn
I have inflamed sores
I want to be alone

Stopping, I step
Outside, trees, flowers, and uncluttered natural space
My head bends back
I stare into the gentle sea in the sky
Come down, sea
Come down, take me up
Up, up, up
But I collapse
Down, body stiffens, then it rests motionless
Come now, turn the lights out, eyes close, body stops

CHAPTER VI : White Hole (Miscellaneous)

I thought I felt ... a tinge of happiness
Like when I gaze down at my beautiful stones of color
Amethyst rose quartz, tiger eye, onyx, and more
Bury me with some of these
Sharp, smooth, diverse, and mine
Bring them with me as I am
Gently placed to rest
In the cool sweet dampness of the earth

My numb soul lingers
My tired soul kisses the gentle spirits
Out of my stones of color
Lifting them to my chest
Held in the embrace of their mother
Pressed to my breast
Are the little spirits of my stones

My soul launches upward
Slowly, gently tugged by the fingers of angels
A loving man with a belly and
Gray hair greets me before the gate
No words need be spoken just yet
Only a long encompassing hug
So long necessary, now fulfilled
I walk with this soldier of war
My throat opens and
My lungs expand
I am overwhelmed with happiness
I *am* Happiness

The loving man with the belly
Talks to me now, like old times, but
Our mouths do not open
Into a sparkling city he takes me

Already waiting, others are
I recognize their love, their eyes, their souls
My animals of past tears already curling around my ankles
Already waiting for me, they were as well
I love them, furry softness
I love them all who are greeting me
I pet the excited spirits at my feet and
Embrace souls with my smiling relatives and friends
I stay close to the loving man with the belly and
He stays close to me
He is my grandfather, guardian, and guide
I am his glamour gal
We are friends

I am overwhelmed with happiness
I am deceased
I have never been so alive
So overwhelmed with happiness and
Afraid not of the cool dampness of the earth
Let it hold me
Let it love me

CHAPTER VII

NARRATIVES OF THE WIND
(Short Stories & Prose)

Banquet of Bliss

Author's Note: Inspired by the play Romeo and Juliet, by William Shakespeare. Written for a high school English class assignment.

"I'm getting old."

My voice had changed into a shaky old woman's. It was not my voice. I was not immobile yet. My feet were slow, but they certainly could move. They wanted to dance.

Inhale, exhale. I rubbed gentle circles around the outside corners of my closed eyes, cursing their taut ridges.

The torches flickered, stinging my reopened eyes with their heat and light. Rapiers dangled from men's belts, glistening like the buttery oils dripping off the moist ham sprawled over the banquet table. I couldn't escape the aroma of sweet edibles; I didn't want to. I inhaled again the scent of dainty meats and luscious fruits. Wine goblets sparkled like golden gems, spread out upon the large table as stars are in the sky. I glanced from the table of savory delicacies toward a young maiden near me who squealed with delight. The jingle of small talk and chuckles echoed through my temples. Everyone acted like young children as they bounced about dancing with one another.

I stood near the banquet table in my new gown of silk brocade. I wanted to eat, but I needed to dance. In my mind I was already pointing my toes and frolicking all over the ballroom.

CHAPTER VII : Narratives of the Wind (Short Stories & Prose)

I couldn't help but admire the smart embroidery of my gloved hands folded in front of me. They suited me quite well and matched the new gown precisely. I swayed gently on my feet, unable to resist the tempting lively spirit of the music. Joy and excitement poured in such abundance that I could not possibly have escaped it, even if I indeed were so inclined.

Shifting my gaze toward the steaming piglets and marinated fish upon the large wooden banquet table, I caught the gaze of an elegantly ornate gentleman. He returned my gawk with a smile. I twitched with warmth and let my eyes glide away from him. The guests moved in vivid flowing motions of dance. As I scampered toward them, holding a part of my dress up with my fingers, I was immersed into a polite embrace. My mouth fell open—I was being held by the man I had exchanged glances with. I gave him a quick nod and the edge of his lips tugged into a smirk of victory.

He led me across the floor on the tips of my toes in the most graceful, fluid manner. He entwined his large fingers through mine and held me like a preciously carved diamond that was worth more than life itself. I gazed up into his eyes. They had taut, deep ridges at the corners, just like mine.

His dark mass of hair reached the tips of his ears, black and midnight blue with sprinkles of gray. He held me in his arms with the firm and gentle skill that an artist might use to grasp his brush. He was solid and muscular, his midsection lacking the paunch of a settled man.

It seemed we danced together for hours. My hands left him as the final note of the exuberant orchestration lingered then faded. Our eyes remained locked. I didn't want to let him go.

"Who are you?" he whispered. "I want to see you again."

"Gillian." The words vibrated dreadfully out of my throat.

I turned away. My heels throbbed in my slippers. My body tugged at me for rest. My stomach begged for the warm ham portions and piglet morsels remaining at the table just a few steps behind.

He took my hand in his. "Your name is almost as beautiful as you are."

"You'll find me at Capulet's house," I volunteered. Why could I not sound so eager?

I drew my hand from his with reluctance; I liked the way our hands felt together. Then I scampered away with such grace as my timeworn legs would let me. I glanced back to him once, only to find him still watching me! A silent promise twinkled in his eyes.

It was a beautiful and most enjoyable ball. Perhaps one night you may attend one for yourself.

Tattoo

"Mama, please let me have this party. I'll be eighteen!"

My mother frowned. "You mean let you have your riot all over this house? I don't think so. I told you before; we can't have all those people in here."

She adjusted her short brown wig and peered into the mirror to check her makeup. Her mauve lipstick rested beautifully against her smooth, pale mocha skin. With her straight wig, she could easily "pass."

When I was much younger, she told me in her level, matter-of-fact tone that back in the sixties she'd had to submit her photo with her college application, she assumed because they needed to confirm she was light-skinned enough to be accepted into her college of choice. She recalled being one of no more than five African American women at the school—all except one nearly lighter than a paper bag. She said the lone dark-skinned student was the smartest black girl she'd ever met. The young woman had been proper, fiercely independent, and particularly tall next to my mother's five-foot-two frame.

I waited. She refused to meet my eyes.

To my mother, conformity was absolutely essential. Deviation from the norm was not allowed. To get ahead, you had to look a certain way, dress a certain way, act a certain way. That was her experience.

I felt it did not have to be my experience.

This had been her last chance. I intended to take advantage of the fact I'd legally be an adult. I was more than capable of finding new opportunities to celebrate my special day that didn't involve her permission. This happened to come in the form of a little permanent body modification.

I'd always wanted this tattoo. I just needed this situation, a push, to get me going.

My boyfriend Tony and I gazed at the large books on the walls. Every page was filled with hordes of tattoos to choose from. From gentle angels to blood-dipped knives, the tattoo shop had enough ideas for anyone who stepped through their doors. I wanted either a flower or a dolphin, finding both choices attractive and feminine. As the pages turned under my searching gaze, a design in the perfect size appeared. The picture fulfilled my desires with a flower and a dolphin beautifully intertwined. I shook in anticipation, yet I browsed slowly through the rest of the large books for procrastination's sake.

Tony spoke Vietnamese with my tattoo artist. He had tattooed one of Tony's friends, so I knew my tattoo would look just as nice. The tattoo artist was bald, but besides that I don't take in much about him except that he was professional, didn't talk much, and focused on his work at hand.

I feigned a sad face in Tony's direction, watching him lean against the door to my small, white-walled tattoo cubical. Slender, handsome, and almost always dressed in Armani Exchange or Banana Republic, he ran his hands through his dyed-blonde hair and tried to reassure me. Tony wasn't allowed to be in the room with me, so said the receptionist. He left after the first five minutes. Apparently, the whole tattoo parlor endured my painful groans. I caught glances of the others watching me twitch and grit my teeth. The tears poured down my face the entire time, but I fought through it.

CHAPTER VII : Narratives of the Wind (Short Stories & Prose)

A couple of buff men who were also getting tattooed teased me playfully. They rooted for my tattoo artist, telling him to poke me harder with the needle because I was moaning as if I liked it. My tattoo artist grinned without looking up and kept concentrating on my upper arm for the next thirty-five minutes. To divert my attention from the pain, I concentrated on my surroundings. One of the buff guys who had teased me earlier was sitting stiff as a board in one of the cubicles across from mine. He was African American with buzzed hair and nice, muscular arms. His gaze was fixed, staring hard into space with his red and watery eyes. He certainly felt pain. He was lucky that he was big, buff, and full of muscle, because the needle wouldn't rattle through a skinny arm and onto his bones like it did mine.

Anyone who says "Tattoos don't hurt at all" or "I never felt it" is lying. If not, they were high during the procedure, trying to practice the art of puffery, or just forgot about the pain—which is highly unlikely. My skin was on fire. Like my cat was using me for a scratching post. It was as if a blind, drunk doctor couldn't find my vein and was stabbing me with his needle a hundred times per second.

Finally, my tattoo guy wiped my arm with a large alcohol pad and spread ointment over my bleeding skin. Despite my throbbing pain, I experienced an excruciatingly surreal euphoria. I couldn't move my legs to stand. I couldn't stop smiling! He wrapped up the area with gauze, explained how to care for it, and sent me on my way. Once I could stand, I walked to the waiting area and waited for Tony to arrive. On the way to the car, Tony opened the passenger door to his dark-green Honda Prelude, helped me inside, and even fastened my seatbelt for me.

He confessed his inability to tolerate my earsplitting screeches.

"I want to hear my song," I said rudely, childlike and pouting, taking advantage of my birthday and how he just wanted to ease my pain and make me happy.

"Okay, honey." He slipped in my new Crazy Town CD and played "Butterfly" on repeat. We listened to the song for the whole twenty minutes it took us to get back to my house.

Tony always catered to my needs and wishes. However, sometimes nice can mean boring. So we'd play a little unspoken game. I'd pretend he'd done something to upset me, just to keep him on his toes. If I dropped my drink on the floor by accident, I'd say, "Tony, why'd you do that?"

"I'm sorry, honey, let me buy you another," he would say as we smiled at each other playfully. He made me feel taken care of. We enjoyed holding hands, going to the mall, and eating out. He was a great listener, laid-back, respectful, and fun to be around. My favorite thing about being Tony's girlfriend was how easy it was to be myself and feel comfortable around him. I loved him.

Our bliss came to an end a few wretched months later. He asked me to marry him in an effort to keep me from leaving. It was the only significant thing we never saw eye to eye on. I didn't see myself leaving him. I just wanted to attend college about four hours away in Virginia. After a few breakups and makeups, he eventually found another girl to dote on—one of his mother's employees at the nail salon where he worked. He threw himself into her to get over me. I dove headfirst into academic study in a vain attempt to heal my heart. We both hurt. Ached for years. But just like the throbbing pain of my tattoo, it eventually subsided, and I almost forgot how bad it hurt those many years ago. Almost.

As time went by, I realized that some people might judge me prematurely because of my tattoo, though others may not. I've heard that I'm sinful or weird. To me, a tattoo is no less odd than getting your ears pierced. People can be hypocrites. They point their proud, vice-gorged fingers despite having three more pointing right back at themselves. Some people never see or even notice my tattoo, while others lean in curiously for a closer look. Most people tell me I'm the last person they thought would have a tattoo, and this makes me feel good.

My mother denying me my party simply sped up the inevitable. When my tattoo finally became a part of my life on my eighteenth birthday, it was ugly. A couple of inches of my left arm resembled how a dry strip of steak might appear after being gnawed with baby teeth and hacked unevenly with a plastic knife. But soon, like a snake, it shed its primitive skin, exposing its true beauty as it matured. I loved it more every day.

The smiling dolphin grew from delicate green leaves with a magenta flower coming from its head. That might sound strange, but it looks lovely. It's soft and smooth, with the smallest traces of texture if you run your fingers across it. It's only three inches long and one inch wide, and to my mother's ongoing dismay, it's not going anywhere.

It's the most adorable little dolphin. This tattoo was worth the suffering, cries, screaming, and shaking. It was also the worst physical pain I had ever felt up until that time. Nothing less than the worst agony I had ever known as it was being borne into this world, becoming a part of me and my life.

My mother doesn't and didn't approve of my lovely and gentle dolphin in bloom. But I also did not approve of my mother rejecting my plea for a huge eighteenth birthday party. The truth was she was still traumatized by my sweet sixteen birthday party, where my friends and I ran wild all over the house and had a blast. Good times, indeed! Nevertheless, I had vowed to make my eighteenth birthday special and memorable. I was an adult now and I needed to symbolize my growth and individuality. Party or not, my day would be special.

A word of advice: going clubbing with friends after a new tattoo is painful!

If I hadn't done it at eighteen, I would have gotten my tattoo sometime later, perhaps when I turned twenty-one. Either way, my tattoo was meant to be.

My mother eventually noticed my little dolphin, but she convinced herself that I had been putting a temporary tattoo on my arm in the same place for the past couple of months. It's safe to say she was in major denial about the change I'd made to my body. My mother was forced to deal with its reality when my, ironically enough, Democratic parents were invited to one of George W. Bush's large inauguration celebrations at a hotel in Washington, D.C. I slipped on a navy-blue spaghetti strap dress that exposed the full beauty of my tattoo. Before we left, I went to my mother's room so she could tell me if I looked okay. She glanced at my upper arm.

"Take off your little picture so we can get out of here. We're going to be late."

"It doesn't come off, Mommy." I referred to her as Mommy instead of my usual Mama to get on her soft side. I didn't like the disappointment in her eyes, so I tried to lighten the mood.

"It likes my arm, Mommy. See?"

I showed it to her, but she only frowned and poked at it.

"Even the dolphin is smiling," I said. "It's happy."

My mother didn't say anything else about it—not to me anyway. When we got in the car, she spoke to my father.

CHAPTER VII : Narratives of the Wind (Short Stories & Prose)

"Did you see what your daughter did to her arm? I hope she can still find a job with that thing sticking to her." She looked back at me. "You know that can't come off, right?"

"Yes, Mommy," was all I managed to say while fighting a laugh.

This exchange made me feel better. My parents knew and didn't send me rolling out of the car and onto the street in my navy-blue dress like I thought they would. My father wasn't upset at all; he was just happy I didn't get some weird piercing or a demon-influenced tattoo on my face. He said so in a half-hearted attempt to lighten the mood and stop his two favorite ladies from fussing at each other. He was looking forward to having a good time at the event, and we were certainly dampening the mood.

When I stepped out of the car and into the fancy hotel, I stood proud of myself, every inch of me. Once inside, I received a few glances at my arm, but no one said a word about it. My tattoo would be a part of me forever; it was time to get used to it. I embraced the pain associated with my tattoo. I figured that to love every inch of myself till the day I died could be an ongoing challenge, but my tattoo had amnesty.

Spark

(DISCLAIMER: Violence, Miscarriage, Torture, Abuse, Cannibalism)

An abused girl's tipping point forces her to seek revenge by telling disgusting lies...

He's drunk. There's no mistaking the off-beat clap of his worn boots against the dirt floor. Heavy-handed, foulmouthed, and bad-spirited, he's like all the men in our Turbid Orilon Lake commune. Endlessly vile.

Mother says Father's good spirit flew away when his first union dissolved. The priest gave him Beth. She died shortly after three stillborn babies fell out of her belly. Two boys and a girl. Mother says when she was given to Father, there was nothing she could do to compete with Beth's memory. Beth and Father's union was arranged as all are, but they had loved each other before the priest had put them together. When Beth died, all the good that was in him died too.

Tonight, Father could have passed out in the pub like last time, but no. Instead, the wooden door shivers against its hinges. The lake splashes a stone's throw outside our door. Startled awake, the water cows with their large dark-brown cyclops eyes groan, murmur and cry like exhausted babies desperate for sleep.

Mother squeezes my arm, her silent warning that I should pretend to sleep. Father is more likely to leave us alone if we ignore him. My little brother, Louis, curls up against Mother's side. We three

CHAPTER VII : Narratives of the Wind (Short Stories & Prose)

have our own cots, but we prefer to push them together, away from Father's cot on the other side of the room.

Father mutters sharp, quick words. He's complaining about our cottage, looking for something. I hear a dull cascade as something falls. Probably wooden cups. Father snorts. I open my eyes. He is strong with ripples of solid muscle surrounded by his protruding belly. Mother's eyes are squeezed shut. I don't know how she manages to cry so hard without making a sound. Mother can do a lot of things I don't understand. She can endure the impossible. Live a lie.

"This place is disgusting."

It was perfectly clean before you started knocking things down. Mother cleaned every single bowl so you wouldn't beat her with them.

"Where is my food?"

You ate it before you went to the pub. What does it matter? If we don't do anything wrong, you just make it up.

I shift my eyes from my mother's face. The twin moons shine bright through a crack in our wooden walls. In a month, the moons will be full. I will be fifteen, and Louis will be eight, as we share a birthday. Mother always says that twin full moons on your birthday are a sign of the divine, bringing good luck.

Father destroys our fragile little kitchen. Throws himself against its walls. Shatters anything he can wrap his hands around.

Where does he get this energy from? He wakes up at dawn like the rest of us.

Silence.

Good. He passes out on the floor. We'll step over him in the morning. There will be no beatings tonight.

"Finish your porridge. Don't be here when he wakes." Mother waves her hands at us. "Get."

My lips tremble. "We don't want you here when he wakes, either," I say.

She holds our faces in her hands and shakes her head. Her eyes are red and tearing. "I'm so sorry. I know. I'll be all right."

"No, you won't," Louis whimpers.

Once she finishes her duties in the cottage, she'll go into the fields like the rest of us. If, that is, Father doesn't render her useless once he finally wakes.

"Besides," she adds, "I need to clean up my special powders." Her hair is thick and wiry, like a tangle of sharp bushes. Her hair pin sticks up sharply like a thorn. One of her crooked teeth protrudes slightly out of her mouth as her lips tremble, but she is beautiful to me. Field soil dusts her coppery-brown skin, smooth and specked with barely visible freckles. "You mean your 'cooking spices'?" I say, brows raised. She's relentlessly secretive about the contents in her special jars.

She shakes her head. "Just go!" She snaps her fingers. She points toward the door, but her eyes tell us she wants another hug.

Louis and I take one last glance at our father's slumped-over frame, wrap our arms around our mother, then rush out the door.

The sun's heat immediately permeates my thin rags. I roll up my flimsy sleeves, and it bathes my skin. "Can I go to school today?" Louis tilts his head and raises his hand over his eyes.

CHAPTER VII : Narratives of the Wind (Short Stories & Prose)

"Go to school. I'll go to the field. If he asks, tell him you worked the field. Father never remembers or notices anything important anyway."

"Okay."

I wrap my arms around his slight frame and hand him a cloth filled with bread, apples and nuts.

"Don't forget. You're the one that has to go to school. When you're old enough, you'll get us out of here." I rub his bald head playfully. Mother recently shaved it when she discovered critters living there. "Remember the places far beyond the lake and mountains?" I ask. "Full towns of women and children who've found asylum. Freedom from the priests and their stupid unions. We're going to get there. We can make it."

"I know." He smiles for the first time all morning. His eyes are green just like mine, but his teeth are crooked like Mother's. I have Father's straight teeth and pale skin. Louis and Mother are brown like the murky lake that runs through our village.

I smile too. The reality of getting away from Father and Turbid Orilon Lake are the only things that could accomplish that feat. That and Richard.

I turn and run away, forcing the thought of Father out of my head. I stop walking as a smell jolts me, making my nose curl. I hate the fields. They reek of human flesh. The priests have too many laws and punishments, and their favorite is death by fire. Men and women burned bloody and black at the stake.

"Yah, I know. It's bad!" Richard shouts as I draw near. "Only fire can burn the Devil out of heretics." He laughs. His thick, long hair sits braided in a flat circle around his head, save for a stray bang that keeps touching his right eye. "Ever since that inquisitor was appointed, we've been getting burned at the stake breaks pretty much every week! One wrong breath and next thing you know, you're up in flames! Should I feel bad that I'm actually happy about it? The breaks from work, I mean."

I love the way the double suns glisten against his hay-colored skin. He's a few months older than me, but he likes when I take charge. He winks at me with his dark-brown eyes and shifts his gaze down to my stomach. I look past him at the deep ditch. The spotted water cows hear his laugher and take the opportunity to beg for food. Richard follows my gaze to the water cows and sprinkles dried hay across the water. They bellow in appreciation. When the water cows saunter out of the lake to sunbathe twice a day, we milk them and pull off the delicious large blue crabs that get tangled into their long matted manes.

"Don't be so loud about it! Best just not say or think anything about it at all." I wrap my dirt-stained faded-green rags tighter around my body with a wry smile. I'm getting noticeably bigger. It was Richard's way to make light of the terrible things that happen around us. To us.

Richard and I share the same type of pain: ruthless assaults from our fathers. Yet we still find joy in each other. Richard is the clearing in my storm. He feels the same about me too. I suppose we are a bit too happy together. I have been with child for many months now.

Richard nods, motions to my womb and reaches for my hand. "Not speaking about things doesn't make them disappear."

I want nothing more than to wrap myself in his arms and feel his strong weight holding me, comforting me. My heart longs for me to be held by him, but my feet force me to step back. Avoid his hand touching mine. I hate my life.

CHAPTER VII : Narratives of the Wind (Short Stories & Prose)

"What's wrong?"

"You want people to see us?" I scold him. "We have to be careful. *You know that*," I whisper, drenched in self-pity.

"I want to be with you! Get out of here. Your mother already knows." He looks at me sternly, pausing until I give him my full attention. "We can't let your father find out. He'll kill you. I'm not willing to let that happen."

I shake my head and hold back tears. "If Father wants to kill me, he will. No one can stop him. I can't leave Mother and Louis. Ever."

"That's my point," he says. His hand tremors. "We need to get out of here because once he knows, it's over. We can take your mother and brother with us. I'm surprised your mother took it so well."

I pick up my large basket and begin filling it with dry hay. "She's more afraid than upset. Keeps making me pray on my knees for forgiveness every chance she gets. She makes me snort some powder mixture. Says it will give me strength for what's to come, or something like that."

"Did you do it?"

"Yah. Of course."

"What is up with your mom and those powders?"

"I don't really know. Don't say anything. Next thing you know, she'll be burning on the stake."

I immediately regret my words. I trust Richard and don't want him to think otherwise. Plus, I feel guilty speaking about Mother that way. With my bad luck, my words will become a reality. Tonight before bed, I'll pray and replace my negative words with better ones.

"Come on, Diana, you know I wouldn't. Even if my mother were alive, I'd still like your mom better. *You know that*," he teases.

I nod and offer a smile. His father strangled his mother to death three years ago. Our commune leadership declared it was her fault. No woman deserved to live if she could not be obedient to her husband. He didn't get in trouble, but the priest didn't put a new wife on him, either.

"You're right. I know." I throw a handful of dry hay in his face. His eyes light up, and he grins.

"Come on!" I shout. "We have to finish the water cows, chickens and pigs."

"I love you. Whatever happens, I'll always be with you." He grabs my basket and covers our faces with it so others can't see if they look our way. I stand on my toes and kiss him.

I stare at the dirt floor with blurry eyes. I can't focus. Blood drips from my face. Is it my nose or my mouth? My stomach aches. Burning. Hurting.

"Who's been at you, Diana? I'm not going to ask again."

I try to answer Father, but sharp words catch jagged in my throat. I cough on my own blood, and my throat hurts from him choking me. I blacked out, but that didn't stop the pain. I can't see, but I can feel everything. I moan and keep shifting my legs. My whole body trembles.

My life slips away with every drop of blood that clots out of me. When I feel myself slip into the afterlife, I scream in my heart as

CHAPTER VII : Narratives of the Wind (Short Stories & Prose)

I fall fast. My baby girl is pressed tightly against my chest; there is no way I'm letting go. Like a stone in a slingshot, something pulls me back before the air pushes out of me, like I have been kicked in the stomach. My baby slips through my fingers and continues to fall. I scream and whimper. Reaching out in vain for my child. I hang there, swinging gently back and forth. My baby falls into the darkness. I can't see her anymore. It's as if there is a thin string holding me between the two worlds, not letting go. The thinnest of threads with an unmatched strength that has been waiting for me. Ready to hold me. Refusing to release my soul into the darkness.

Mother sits with me, my head on her lap and my legs curled under me as she strokes my hair. At dawn, my mother's scream raised me from my bizarre revelations. I notice that a large puddle of blood developed under me and stained my pale legs.

"My heart burns." I cry. I can hardly hear my own words.

Father wakes, but he only stares at us. Mother shouts at Louis to go fetch Mrs. Anna, who is the midwife. Father leaves and drags Louis with him.

"Your girl-child has gone to Heaven," Mrs. Anna explains. "The Lord is merciful." She touches my hair gently.

I look away from Mrs. Anna to the tiny, bloody and limp baby in my arms. I hold her as long as my mother will let me. The baby has a birthmark over her eyebrow. She is so precious.

"He blessed you by granting your prayers. Took away what would have been an extra mouth to feed," she whispers confidently, patting me on the head.

I never prayed for that.

"Get some rest. Drink lots of water." She withdraws, nods to my mother and smiles at me before leaving. "You'll be all right."

"I want my baby," I whine with a groan, turning my head from left to right.

"You'll have more babies," Mother says gently.

"I don't want more. I want this one," I cry.

"Then pray. Take this," she says, opening her hand.

We pray together, then I snort every pinch of powder from her palm.

I sleep for a long while. When I wake, Mother is standing over me with a large bowl of soup.

"That smells great. Where's mine?" Louis asks. He peers into the bowl. "That looks like meat! We haven't had any in as long as I can remember."

"Sweetheart, this is a special soup just for your sister," Mother says as she lifts the spoon to my chapped lips. "To help her feel better." I accept the spoon and swallow the finely cut, tender chunks. I look past her to our small kitchen. Three of her special powders are open and sitting on the wooden counter. The smooth brown walls of our cottage are rotted and unstable, dark with patches of mold.

My eyes open wide. This was delicious.

CHAPTER VII : Narratives of the Wind (Short Stories & Prose)

"That's not fair," he says.

"I can share, Mother." My voice comes hoarse. "Who gave us meat? That was nice of them." My throat hurts, and the warm liquid is soothing against it. "Louis, come here."

"No!" Mother says sharply, shooing him away. She pauses and regains her composure, speaking gently, "This is Diana's. Louis, your supper is still warm. It's over there wrapped in the plantain leaves." She motions towards it. He obeys.

The cot is cold against my skin. I cover myself with a thin blanket and wring my hands. Clasp them so hard that it hurts. I pray—no, beg—God to make my father leave us alone. I rub my upper arms for comfort and hug my shoulders. I stop fighting the memories. Memories of dark ghosts in my father's form, yanking my hair and cursing me. Unable to speak or just muttering to myself, I want to die. I need the pain to end.

I'm overwhelmed with an insatiable itch that steals my hot tears, dissolving them into a dark cloud with grotesque red and black veins. A wicked, floating, vaporous threat full of blood and lightning that strikes and soaks me dripping wet. Shocked and steaming, my heart frazzled, soul scorched.

A voice vibrates against my ears as it crawls from dark corners, resting under my cot and singing from my pillow. A pleading voice that lets loose in the shadow of the moonlight. Rocking me awake with a ferocious melody. A harmonious tune of desperation, protection and survival.

Confusion hurls my mind in different directions. My heart grieves without peace, full to the rim with burnt ashes. I'm so angry I can hardly breathe.

Eventually, a realization burns my heart and pushes into my veins: the inevitable infinity song that has no end will continue to haunt me unless I submit and create the final notes myself.

This bright light of awareness surges through me from the grisly lightning cloud in Heaven's sky. I'm given a new heart, and it's like it's cut from the chest of the supreme God herself. I'm no longer frazzled and brutalized but starving and powerful.

There's a throbbing ache in my core—fiery heat. Finally, I bring forth my voice. My own dark song. A scream. I crave the feel of my baby in my arms. I want to smell her. Touch her. Kiss her little feet!

At dawn, Father drags me toward the door, forcing me off my feet. I collapse. I don't care what he's doing. It can never be worse than what he has already done.

"You always give me a hard time," he sighs, shaking his head. He blinks one eye, and sweat falls into it. His upper eyelid is droopy, nearly covering his whole eye. "What's your problem?"

"You," I sneered.

"Didn't you hear Dulcitius of Marburg?" His voice is sharp. "Everyone has their part. When you quit, it affects all of us. I can't stand when everyone complains about you."

"Really?" I scoff, throwing my head back. "I don't care what that inquisitor says. None of them care about us. They want us afraid. On our knees." I'm so drunk with disdain that my next words shoot out of my throat. Piercing the air like the cries of those at the stake as the first lick of the flames mauls their toes.

CHAPTER VII : Narratives of the Wind (Short Stories & Prose)

"You mean, when I quit, it affects *you*. We pick up *your* slack when you're drunk and can't work. Now you have to work like the rest of us." My eyes widen, and my fear sheds away like a snake's skin. A poisonous snake.

I push myself upright. "They don't complain about me; *you* complain to them about me. About all of us!" An irresistible urge to argue comes over me. "I know the truth. Your whole reality is a lie."

"You. Your mother. Both of you don't see what's around you. Barely enough of anything for anyone. Half-rotted crops. Witches and demons always trying to trick us." He waves his hand into the air. "Whatever we've done wrong, we need to fix it. With the help of Dulcitius of Marburg, we will. We must keep praying that God stops punishing us. She's already taken away my family. I don't need you, your mother and even Louis to mess up more than we already have. All of you just keep God's wrath on me. I can't take any more."

He clasps and unclasps his hands, shaking his head down at me.

"If God has already taken away your family, who are *we*?" I open my arms wide. A laugh curls out of my mouth and slaps him in the face.

He hits me. The blow knocks my eyes shut. Once I open them, I feel like I have poisonous venom. It oozes from my belly into my throat, boils over and shoots out through my eyes. If he would just look at me, I know my glare would kill him.

Father is like a worn-out rag doll, the kind we make with straw and mud from the lake. He has no words left, only slumped shoulders and unwilling eyes. Suddenly, he stalks out of the cottage, almost tripping over himself as if he couldn't get away from me fast enough. I know the painful ache of his blows will follow me for hours. The one on my face and the other deep in my heart. Being together as a family with Father would be impossible. I have always felt this way, but now I am certain.

I stumble back to my cot. I rest my cheek onto my pillow, careful not to bother the swollen side. I raise my hand to my face; its trembling. My pillow is singing to me again. It's an unsavory song but soothes my fear and commands me to change the path of my life.

As my pillow's song quiets, I imagine Mother and Louis far off tending the water cows. That is my job. I do need to get to work, regardless of what Father says. No more water cows, not now. There's a different job I must do. I wince when I hear the door slam.

"You whore!" Richard's father, Mr. Kempe, spits, glowering at me. His lips are curled, and droplets of sweat decorate his thick brows. I push myself off my cot and cower against the wall. There is nowhere to hide.

"I pulled your father off of Richard today. This is all because of you." He comes at me. "How dare you corrupt my son. I will send you to hell!"

My fear breaks into sharp pieces at my feet, and the heat in my veins bubbles over. I stare daggers into him. Tearing him to shreds with my eyes, daring him to come closer. There's no room for the self-pity of my past; it was sliced out and bled to death over an open flame. Only hunger, power and change can come into my nightmare. They will wake me up.

Finally, Mr. Kempe hits me. He wraps his hands around my neck; he's hurting me. I swing and punch blindly all around. My fists ache sharply each time they slam against his pudgy frame. I'm strong. I'm angry. I'm crazy. I'm going to kill him!

All of a sudden, he stops, and I'm still swinging. I can hardly see him. His weight lifts off of my cot, and I consider going after him. My

CHAPTER VII : Narratives of the Wind (Short Stories & Prose)

knuckles ache, and I'm breathless, so I don't. My eyes swell, foggy with tears, but I see him now. With a distorted face and busted lip, he spits at me. He runs into the wooden meal table, stumbles back, then lunges forward out of the door. I'm so glad Richard is nothing like his father. As I am nothing like mine—at least, I don't think so. I remain the rest of the day in my bed, cheeks soaked with silent tears.

It's the strangest thing not to be able to speak with Richard. He was caught hanging around my cottage waiting for a chance to sneak in and see me. This is why Father and Mr. Kempe believe I have been with Richard to make my baby. I could hear Richard limping outside. Richard swore to them that he was concerned about me because of our friendship, but they knew better. Father forbade me to see him, and his father forbade him the same. Mother has taught me how to write a few things and play with small numbers, so it didn't stop me from scribbling a note to him. I wrote that I had a plan to change everything. To make things right. I wrote that he must destroy the note in the murky lake after reading it. A few weeks ago, someone was sent to the stake for protecting runaway heretics. Like Richard, I actually look forward to the executions. Everyone in our commune is given a break from our labor and made to watch.

With this in mind, I make my way to Dulcitius of Marburg's house. I should be frightened to confront him, but I'm more excited than anything else. Each step I take toward the inquisitor's house, my grin grows more wicked.

Every stone under my feet pinches me. My sandals are thin and worn. With each step, the dry brownish-green dirt kicks up and threatens my eyes. The heat of the two suns slowly cuts deep into my shoulders. I rub them gently. It's nothing compared to my life's horror—the life father thrust on us. I'm not afraid of these memories anymore. They'll give me the strength to change my life.

My eyes begin to ache, and I rub them. Despite the painful throb in my head, I see the sprinkle of slender, curvy trees with their naked branches marking my path. Fruit and leaves hardly last on our trees. We are all so desperate to pick every fruit and rip away any leaves in which to wrap around our food for steam cooking over fire pits.

Guards stop near the inquisitor's door, and I feel as pitiful and miserable as I ever have. A thick man with broad shoulders and filthy hair leers at me. His voice breaks as he speaks.

"What's wrong with you, little wench?" He grabs his groin and shakes his pockets. "Papa making you earn extra coins before letting you come home for supper?" He snickers at me. "I can help with that."

This guard doesn't have any teeth. I shake my head in denial and flinch at the sudden sound of rough footsteps coming near me.

"Dulcitius of Marburg isn't receiving anyone, girl." The second guard appears as he invades my personal space to stand in front of me; I instinctively take a few steps back.

I simply bore my eyes into both of them. I must look like a fool. Dirty blond knots for hair, teary green eyes, wearing a bucket of rags with sandals.

"He will receive me." My voice quivers. I walk past the toothless guard, but he grabs my shoulder. His hand rips open the sunburned skin there. I holler and tear myself away from his grip. I use the pain in my voice to make my declaration more believable. "He will see me. My father is a demon, and if I do not see Dulcitius, our whole village will be cursed!"

CHAPTER VII : Narratives of the Wind (Short Stories & Prose)

The second guard spits on the dirt and walks toward the entrance of the lair. The guard's eyes widen, then narrow. He turns around, and I follow him inside. I shiver, and I feel dizzy. I don't want to be anywhere near these two men. I'm not given a choice to sit, so I stand. Slow and heavy footsteps clank loud like the beaten copper bell in the middle of our village square.

I wipe sweat from my eyes with my flimsy sleeve as a cloaked figure comes toward me. The cloaked man is thin. His eyes are wrinkled and somber. Patches of dark curls pepper his balding head. He shouts as if I'm in another room instead of standing right before him. "Who is the heretic?"

"M...My father. He forces sin onto our family and worships the Devil every night."

The inquisitor looks at me warily. "Why only now is it that you confess this?"

I shoot back, "I am afraid! He has become more and more vicious. At first, he only conversed with demons. Now I believe he is becoming one!"

He motions for the guards to leave the room. I watch as he slithers onto a fancy stool, and his robe flows past his knees, completely covering his feet. "Tell me what you know. I'll have the three high priests preside over this case."

I tell him lies of my father's heresy, making sure to include Mr. Kempe's partnership in it all. His guards order me to lead them to my home. Father isn't there, so they follow me to the pub. People turn and stare at us as we walk together. They know death is coming. No sooner do I point out my father than they drag him, arms flailing and lungs wailing, to the town dungeon. Two of the guard's curse and take off in the direction of Mr. Kempe's cottage.

I stand and watch until I'm surrounded by silence. Father's broken sandals are strewn in the dirt. I explain in detail to Mother about the toothless guard because I'm particularly afraid of him. She kisses my forehead, holding me in her comforting arms. She tells Louis that I am the blessing we have been praying for.

"Something sparked in you, Diana. You're letting it change you. Take you over," Mother said.

I shake my head. My lips narrow, and the corners of my mouth turn downward. Dulcitius of Marburg sent his servants to notify the commune that we are to meet in the courtyard in the morning. We all will be required to watch the trial. For some reason, I assumed Father would be burned at the stake, which always happens in the field. When they tell us to meet at the courtyard, that usually means they're going to torture the accused on the large wooden stage or boil them alive in an oversized cauldron.

"Why are they taking Father to the courtyard instead of the field?" I ask.

Mother pauses in thought before putting away the last of our wooden bowls on a shelf. "I think because he's being tried for more than just heresy. You said he raped, murdered and spoke with demons, right?"

"I can stop this. Tell them I don't remember anything anymore."

Mother bites her lip and shakes her head, her breath quickening. "Why? You feel sorry for your father? Have you finally found some love in your heart for him?"

CHAPTER VII : Narratives of the Wind (Short Stories & Prose)

"I always had love for him." I pause and correct myself. "I always had hope. You know, that he could love us back. At least not hate us. That things could be different."

I glance to Mother, then to Louis who is resting on his cot, carving a water cow out of a piece of wood.

Mother shakes her head. Her hands are busy cleaning the cottage. She stops and looks right at me as her rag falls to the floor. "Don't fight it," she says, her hands trembling. "Don't push down your anger. Your pain. Don't be like me." Her voice strains. "Don't you see where it got me? I can't get away from him. What type of a mother am I?" She twitches, and I can tell she is fighting back tears. "I can't protect my own children."

I don't remember ever seeing her so wretched.

"My greatest fear is that you and Louis will see what a dull coward I am. Hate me for what I've done. What I couldn't do." She wipes her brow and lets her tears fall.

"Your father got dealt a losing hand. I was put onto him." She nods, then pauses, wipes her sleeve across her face. "Uglier and more senseless than his first wife."

I open my mouth to speak, but she holds up her hand, silencing me. She shouldn't talk about herself like this. None of this is her fault. A wife has no protection against a husband's will.

"If he had gotten a better deal, he would have been a better man. A better father. He's not a bad person."

"Not a bad person?" I break in. "You know what he's done. To all of us. To my baby." My voice trails, and heat rises from my core.

"When bad things happen to good people, they can change," Mother says, her voice higher pitched. "I saw that in your father's eyes. I see it in you, now."

"What does that mean? I don't understand what you want me to do."

"I'm not going to make your decisions. You are strong."

"No, I'm not."

"But you are. You can be." Her tears stop, and she meets my gaze. She pushes a frizzy lock of hair behind her ear. "I can't fix my mistakes. "I'll be damned, though, if I watch you make the same."

She comes toward me and opens her arms. I fall into them. I need her. Despite everything, I never doubt my mother's love for me. I am never sure, though, if she loves herself.

"I want you to do better than me. Be better," she whispers and kisses the top of my head. "Don't you ever let anyone put out that spark in you. Control you." She squeezes me and gives me a shake. "Do anything but be like me."

She holds me away and tilts my head up with the palm of her hand. "All I know is fear and love. Fear of everything and love for you and your brother." She wipes a tear from my eyes with her thumb. I didn't realize I was crying.

"You've got to know more than me! Know some courage. Know some faith." She pauses, then says coldly, "To know when to stop feeling sorry for those who don't deserve it."

CHAPTER VII : Narratives of the Wind (Short Stories & Prose)

Clad in a short black robe that falls to the tops of his knees, one of the executioners, Mr. Tackie, strips Father naked and dry-shaves him. Says it makes discovering the Devil's mark less tedious. When not torturing and executing people, Mr. Tackie fixes boots and shoes next door to the blacksmith.

The weight of the stares makes me tremble. I'm supposed to speak. In a ferocious storm of tears and determination, I explain what my father and Mr. Kempe have "done." The other executioners are eager to get their hands on him. I can't speak fast enough. They quickly wave me away and prick Father with the thick, blunt needle of a bodkin. His shoulders look dislocated, probably from having them pulled up behind his back. His hip joint is forced from its socket. We watch as Mr. Kempe's toenails are torn out with turcas. We are careful not to show too much compassion lest someone think we sympathize with Devil worshipers. Father's one eye is gouged out, while the other is burned out of its socket. His front teeth extracted with pliers. He spits onto the floor every time the raw sockets fill with blood.

I stand close to Richard as we look across the crowd of people from the high stage, then shift our gazes back to look at Mr. Kempe slumped over next to Father. Mother is in the back somewhere with Louis. I can't see her. She doesn't want to watch, but everyone is required to be present during these punishments.

I look at Richard's hand, and I want to hold it—but I can't. Not yet. Richard has wrapped his arms around himself as if it can stop him from shaking. He keeps his head down so he doesn't have to see his father suffering. It doesn't matter. All of us can still hear it. There is no escape.

I notice Mr. Kempe's blotched and red skin from when he was forced to take a scalding hot bath laced with lime, which sears the flesh. The priest gets our attention and makes sure we watch as Mr. Kempe's right foot is covered with lard and roasted slowly over the fire until his bones crack and pop as the marrow drips onto the flames.

"Is that all you have left to say, young lady?"

I look each priest in the eye. One is tall, one fat, and the other so short his feet don't touch the ground as he sits. They wear robes and strange pointed hats.

"Yes. It's the same as before, your grace. My Father worships the Devil."

I pause, and they watch me, clearly waiting for more information.

"He told me the demons said he must commit sins against God in order to win their favor. To be a head Devil priest, he had to commit sin by incest. Father raped me." I know it is a lie, but in my heart, it's true. The tears start to come again. My reliable, grief-stricken tears.

"He would kill me if I told," I say. "But I trust God. I know the Lord. She will protect me for speaking the truth."

I shift from one foot to the other. "When he found out I was pregnant, he beat me in hopes of killing the child so there'd be no evidence. A few days after that, he sent Mr. Kempe into our cottage to break the law of union and morality by raping me too. That the sin would please the Devil!"

"Yes," the heavy-looking priest says. He leans to the side, and the chair creaks. I can't understand how it continues to hold his weight.

"The witness, your neighbor, said she saw Mr. Kempe come into your house on the same day you said."

CHAPTER VII : Narratives of the Wind (Short Stories & Prose)

"Yes, your grace." I wipe sweat from my face. The suns bite at me with their rays. We have been out here all morning. Father gets silenced each time he offers an explanation. He denies wrongdoing, and they continue to torment him with questions and pain.

"And you, boy," the same priest says. "Do you have anything else to add?"

Richard shifts his weight from one foot to the other, then shakes his head, silent.

What does it matter? The servants are already bringing in a large bowl filled with rats. The priests are going to torture them regardless of anything else we say. They mean to turn the bowl onto their bare stomachs and light a fire over the top. I've seen this once before. The rats panic and burrow into their bowels. It would take a while for Father and Mr. Kempe to die from the rats, but they would feel the pain immediately.

The dry, rotted stage creaks again as I glance at my feet. My slippers are blood-stained, the soles soaked. My nose keeps curling at the stench. I'm not sure if Father or Mr. Kempe soiled themselves or if it's the stink of their insides connecting with the air.

"So he tried to put the blame on you. That you impregnated the girl?" the tall priest asks Richard.

"She and I are friends," Richard mumbles. "We would never think about sinning." His voice cracks, and he wrings his hands. "We're not married. Too young to know of these things you're talking about."

Richard and I return to our work tending the water cows. The church takes a little of the money my father had. Father's debtors are too afraid to acknowledge any relationship with him, so we are permitted to keep the rest. Everything else we had didn't mean anything. I scan our small cottage: flimsy cots, tattered towels and dented wooden cups.

Mother is filling a bag with her spices by wrapping the delicate containers with the cushion of our raggedy clothes.

"What's going on?" I ask, but I already know.

"In the last few months, I've been praying and sprinkling blessings," she says without looking at me. "But it's not safe. Never will be. In Turbid Orilon Lake, everyone will burn to their death. By fire or by sorrow."

I nod, pick up an empty potato sack and start shoving my clothes into it.

"Your father had it coming. If we stay here, we will too. It will be our fault."

She shakes her head. "When I prayed, the holy spirits told me that the priests will never let you marry Richard. They said they're going to marry you to the toothless guard in the spring. I'll end up someone's third wife. Louis will be an unwanted stepchild. There's nothing good for us here."

The thought of being the toothless guard's wife causes my limbs to tense. "Absolutely, never ever!"

Mother nods in agreement, and Louis raises his head as if to check if I'm all right.

CHAPTER VII : Narratives of the Wind (Short Stories & Prose)

"Louis hasn't finished his education yet. How can we take care of ourselves?" I ask.

"I don't know," she says, opening and closing her hands in frustration. "All I know is the holy spirits say we aren't safe. We've got to leave immediately. We listen to God, and she will take care of the rest."

"Are we going to the towns beyond the lake and mountains? I don't want to raise my child here." I place my hand over my belly.

"Your child?" Her largest crooked tooth pokes out as she smiles.

When my daughter is placed in my arms, my mouth falls open and I squeal. It feels good to have my husband, Richard, at my side and our daughter in my arms. I never regret my past, what I did. I embraced my time for revenge and lied with a confident heart. Yet God found it in her heart to have mercy on me.

"She's back!" I shout, squeezing my eyes shut and opening them again.

I have seen her face before! I know my baby. The exact same little eyes and nose. The same birthmark over her eyebrow. My girl-child did not go to Heaven. Her spirit left the old body, yes—but stayed with me, only to return right back in my womb. All is finally well.

I take in a deep, satisfying breath and nod to my beloved Richard. He rubs my back and kisses my cheek. My mother hums faintly as she pours warm stew into a wooden bowl for me. It is hearty with beans, corn and barley. I watch Louis play with a soft toy made of braided hay in the corner of the room. A few days earlier, we celebrated my birthday along with his tenth one. We have found a new commune beyond the lake and mountains where we were welcomed with open arms. They helped us build two cottages side by side. Mother took up work as a medicine woman and healer, so we are able to get by while Louis goes to go to school every day. Richard and I quickly found ourselves working alongside the water cows, like old times but better. Water cows are such large and gentle creatures, but if you don't feed, water and pet them enough, they will bite your ankles and drag you drowning into the water. Most are too afraid to tend them, but Richard and I can't get enough of them.

A warm, soothing sensation takes hold of me. Is this what peace feels like? I shift my gaze back to the child in my arms. I hold her close, lean down and inhale. She smells like an enchanting angel. Her scent does something powerful to me. She smells the way beauty and purity might if they could be laid into a barrel and churned with a plunger, like how we whip milk to make butter. I touch the fine hair of her head. I run my knuckles along her delicate cheeks. I kiss her little feet.

The End.

Eternity

Why was I trembling over the deep pit of fire, staring in? Hot air from the flames stung my eyes like a lemon squeeze gone wild.

A soft hand gripped my shoulder. One of the angels leading my wretched group gazed at me with the most compassionate expression. Shaking his head slowly, he tightened his grip on me just enough to clarify that I wasn't going anywhere but in.

Before I knew it, someone caught my arm and tossed me into the pit. Clawing at the air and screaming, I managed to latch onto the edge. I wasn't going down without a fight; this was a mistake! I hadn't been the best Christian woman, but I was a Christian for my whole life. This was not right!

Fear ripped through me, but out of curiosity I peered downward. The drop was far, yet I could see clearly to its bottom. The souls landed without a thud, stood right back up, and were led away by dark-haired demons with sculpted, firm bodies. No, they were angels. Demons couldn't possibly look so attractive. Angels held onto their arms and, in most cases, literally dragged the souls away. These angels were no less shining and beautiful than the angels above the pit, but they had a wickedness about them. They didn't touch the human souls with the tenderness of the angel who had touched me. They were rougher and impatient.

Grabbing one stone after another, I pulled myself upward until I could see light from where I had been thrown. The shape of the hole was crooked, so I couldn't maneuver myself the way I needed to pull myself out. I strained to peer above the hole where a few scattered angels were roaming about. They were too far away to hear me. Even if they did, they would probably toss me back in. I didn't care, of course. I had to try. "Help! Someone, please! This is a mistake! Someone, help! Help, please!" I hollered.

Muscles shaking, I almost lost my grip, but I had found a stone where I could rest my left foot. I had never stopped panicking, and the heat from below was making my fingers perspire. I wouldn't be able to hold on.

I wept and turned my head downward again to find another foothold for my right foot, but there was none in sight. I couldn't see well; my tears blinded me. No way was I going to remove my hands from the stone to wipe them.

"Hey, there!" Snickering followed this shout. "You might as well let go. We'll have you either way. God promised you to us when he sent the Light Ones to bring you. Save yourself the hassle. Come on down! Don't be afraid." A rumble of awful laughter followed. Five or so dark angels surrounded the speaker, laughing and pointing at me. It was amazing such a sadistic tone could come from something so beautiful. I couldn't make out his face very well, but his loveliness was immense. I could sense it rather than see it specifically. The dark ones around him shared his same beauty, yet they were different in facial features. I wasn't giving in to their taunts. I looked up again, trying to peer over the ledge. No one was even faintly near.

"The Lord is my shepherd; I shall not want! He leadeth me in the green pastures and lie me by the still waters. He restoreth my soul!" I had to think for a moment, trying to remember the rest. Was I even saying it right? They continued to laugh at me.

CHAPTER VII : Narratives of the Wind (Short Stories & Prose)

One of them yelled up, "Even I know Psalms 23! If I know it and I'm still here, what makes you think it's going to save you?"

Every word was accompanied by the deep belly laughs of his companions. I didn't care. I tried to remember. "He anoints my head with oil, my cup runs over me! Yea though I walk through the valley of the shadow of death, I will fear no evil: for you are with me; thy rod and thy staff comfort me!" I cried, my words falling into each other. I knew it wasn't perfect, but what else was I to do?

"Oh, please," another angel said, sarcasm bleeding over his lips. They grew quiet and began talking amongst themselves.

"Shut up, my friend," another said. "I'll go and get her."

Murmurs, soft laughs and whistles directed toward me filled my ears. One angel took off his vest, revealing a muscular chest. He never took his eyes off me as he stripped. He climbed up the stones toward me. Didn't all angels have wings? Why didn't he just fly up to get me? Was he taking his time to watch me suffer? He drew closer and his long, blackish-blue hair and deep blue eyes glowed in the semidarkness. His smile was fixed and hard, almost mechanical.

"Jesus!" I cried out, gazing over the ledge. My whole body quaked and my head throbbed. I looked down and saw that he was still taking his time. His grimace remained unchanged. Looking up again, I cried out, "God, I believed in you and Jesus! I was never perfect, but please! I prayed to you, I..." I looked down again, monitoring his progress. My left foot ached from supporting my weight. I cried out toward the light above me.

"I believe Jesus died for our sins! I believe in the Father, the Son, and the Holy Ghost, I...I mean Spirit!" I stuttered. Tears had resumed with a fierceness I couldn't comprehend. With my scratchy, fear-streaked voice, I sang a Gospel song I loved, "Awesome God." I sniffled. I couldn't remember the exact words from my random church excursions, but my body had stopped shaking despite my panic, and I was able to continue.

I couldn't remember all of the verses except that main chorus I liked. I didn't even know the whole song when I was alive. I was mildly comforted by the sound of my own scratchy voice. I always loved this song because it had a beat I could dance to and the words were simple and strong. I clapped along to my voice, like the Easter Sundays back in church when I was a little girl. I imagined I could even hear the chorus of my old church, and the music seemed right next to my ears.

I gasped when I realized I'd been clapping and not holding myself up. Yet somehow my right foot had found leverage.

In the middle of the chorus I screamed, more out of shock than fear. The dark angel had wrapped his hand around my ankle. His long nails dug into my skin. I stopped singing, but the music still rang in my ears. My hands flew out to claw at the ledge. The dark angel tightened his grip, tugging me viciously. My grip couldn't compete with his strength and my fingers dragged mercilessly off the rock, but I didn't fall. Someone above was clasped tightly to my arm, right above my elbow. I was being pulled in two directions!

My body shook. I looked up at the hand that held onto my arm; it was a male hand. I gazed up past the wrist to his neck and a face emerged. Light green eyes, the shade of the inside of a lime fruit met my gaze. He had full wavy locks of dark green, just barely past his shoulders. I could see the beginnings of a shirt, from some gossamer material I couldn't name, but it was white with small golden dots resembling buttons. He wasn't looking at me; he looked past me at the beautiful dark angel.

CHAPTER VII : Narratives of the Wind (Short Stories & Prose)

"Hello, brother," the angel with the green eyes said with impressive firmness and determination.

The dark-haired angel's smile crumbled away like the ashes of burnt wood. His voice was harsh. He growled, "Damn you, slave of God! She's mine."

The angel on my arm shook his head with a kind smile. "God heard this woman's soul. She is no longer yours to torment." He spoke with clear authority. The angel with green hair finally met my eyes and smiled. He pulled me toward him, but the angel of hell had yet to release his grip on my ankle. My savior angel shifted his gaze back to the dark one, speaking plainly and firmly again. "In the name of God, release her, Lorcan. She is his child and is no longer under your authority."

The dark angel let go of my ankle and pushed himself from the stones of the pit. He floated down slowly, leveraged by his half-open black wings.

My green savior pulled me up easily, as if I weighed no more than a feather. I cried. My angel pulled me against him and held me. Soaking in the comfort of his arms for a good while, I imagined time had little significance here in heaven. *Is this heaven?* I thought. It didn't matter yet. Every time he stroked the length of my straight, jet-black hair, my sobs softened. He squeezed me for a moment then released the pressure with his arms still around me.

His lithe form and delicate jawline drew my attention. His light green eyes watched mine until I lowered my gaze. The taut muscular definition of his spiritual body flirted with my eyes on the way down. His skin—flushed golden with a soft brilliant glow—begged to be touched through his thin shirt. He wore cloud-white pants with shoes of flexible gold. He was an angel, but I didn't see any wings. *Angels are supposed to have wings.*

I was rude to stare, but it was impossible not to. My eyes were still moist from crying. I drew my mouth into a straight line and bit my lip.

"I thought people couldn't cry in heaven," I mumbled.

He wiped my eyes with his hands, smoothing away hair that had stuck itself to the wetness of my face. "Child of God, you are not in heaven yet."

"Where am I, then?" I wasn't worried or frightened. Just confused and thankful.

"The plane between heaven and hell."

My brow rose.

"On Earth, some call it purgatory."

My eyes widened and a shiver went up my spine. I ground my teeth. "So I'm not in heaven yet?" *I need to get to heaven. I can't be here. Not here.*

"You have already been saved. I've got you."

I met his eyes and nodded in gratitude. His hair was green, just like his eyebrows and lashes. His freckles were almost too faint to notice. He was beautiful. *How am I attracted to him when I'm only a spirit? Am I lusting?*

He smiled shyly and turned his face away, looking toward the large Golden Gate. God wasn't going to throw me back into the pit for lusting, was he? The stench still clung inside my nose—like roasting flesh.

CHAPTER VII : Narratives of the Wind (Short Stories & Prose)

Moments ago I had been led into a separate line, the one that didn't lead toward the Golden Gates. A sick tingling sensation stuck onto me as droplets of sweat broke out over my skin. I had stood still, trying my best not to keep up with the line until one of the angels pushed me along with the gentle pressure of his palm.

"There's been a mistake," I had said, trying to sound as controlled and confident as possible. "Where am I going?"

My eyes suddenly blurred and things shook and distorted around me. I was weak. My angel caught me in his arms, but they felt like wings, I didn't know.

"Are you all right?"

"No. I can't stop thinking about what happened. Can we leave? Anywhere but here." I motioned toward the pit and coughed.

"Yes," he said softly, still holding me in his arms. "I am taking you to the gate over there. The entrance to heaven."

He gave me a reassuring squeeze. "I'm Alaric. Come on now, Jung Hwa."

How did he know my name? Never mind; he's an angel. He knows my name. It's also obvious that he also knows what I'm thinking. My fingers entwined in the hand he held out for me. I felt secure holding his hand like this. It would be a long walk to the Gate. There were hordes of souls waiting in line to see if their names were listed in the Book of Life. I forced myself to smile and walked, holding onto Alaric's hand with one hand while with the other I clung to the bottom of his elbow, clasped onto him like a child. He was tall—I was about five-foot-three, so I guessed him to be close to six feet tall. He was soft, warm, and of flesh. A faint glow of light surrounded him. An unmistakable brilliance.

I tore my gaze from Alaric to take in my surroundings. Everything was white and blank. Something was growing tall and wide and colorful that you might call trees, but there wasn't anything I could call a sky or the ground. Now that I was far from it, I wanted to look back and see the pit I had come from, but I was afraid I might turn into a pillar of salt or something. I wasn't taking any chances! I imagined smoke would be rising from that pit filled with hell's fire. Fire and angels.

They all looked beautiful, even the bad ones. Earlier, when I was being marched toward the pit along with a group of other unfortunates, some screamed and others simply cried. It obviously led to somewhere we knew we didn't want to go. The last soul in line, I stood with sweaty palms watching as someone jumped in, sadly without protest. Another screamed, cried and cursed. *That's hell*, I thought. *This is a mistake!* I had glanced around frantically, deciding that, though it might be in vain, I was going to try to make a run for it.

I blinked and shook my shoulders, hoping to break loose of this memory. The tips of my fingers twitched nervously from my close encounter with hell. *Stop thinking about it. Stop.*

I took a deep breath and focused on Alaric's warm arm under my hands. He was the present, here and now. Far away ahead, the beginnings of a sky cascaded in a beautiful ripple of pastel violet and white that began after the high Golden Gates. Two large entrances of golden fences both long and wide reached farther than I could see. Everything was beautiful except I couldn't block out the crying in front of me. A large group wept as they were led to the pit by the same angels who had previously led me. They were going to hell. I didn't want to look at them. One almost touched me, but I tightened my grip on Alaric. He let go of my hand to set his arm around my shoulders. His arms must have been designed for the

CHAPTER VII : Narratives of the Wind (Short Stories & Prose)

sole purpose of comforting me. He was warm and smelled like crisp fresh air from the sea.

He and I were silent for a while. Curiosity bubbled up into my chest with each moment that passed. Can he tell me more about Purgatory? What was heaven like?

"So," I said.

He looked at me.

"If there are no tears in heaven, does that mean everyone is perfectly happy? You know...no problems, sickness, trouble, and stuff?"

He smiled and looked toward the gates, never stopping his feet. "We are happy here. It is not a perfect happiness, though, because there can be problems or worries. Sickness and sadness have no place. There is no room for the annoyances and responsibilities of your previous life. No bills to pay, rent, or school expenses. Everything is prepared for you, without taking away the joys of your previous life. So much more is added."

"You mean prepaid?"

"Yes. Prepared and prepaid. Your behavior and faith while in the life of the flesh determines your heavenly home and honorarium reward."

I grimaced. "Then I think I may just have a shack. Probably in the ghetto of heaven living an eternity on spiritual food stamps."

He squeezed my hand, his lips tugging into a genuine smile. "Better a shack in heaven than a mansion in hell, yes?"

He chuckled. His laugh was the true definition of angelic. He was absolutely adorable. I wanted to be serious, though. Would I live in the ghetto? I didn't want to think about it anymore.

"Tell me about God. How does he look?" We continued to walk together in the pure white blankness toward the gates.

His eyes brightened while he spoke about his heavenly Father. His tone was of love and truth, if love and truth are a tone. He spoke reassuringly and proudly—in a way I could never doubt any word he said.

"God does not have a 'look,'" he said. "He has a feel and a sound. A touch. He has these in such abundance that there is no need for more. God can take any form that pleases him. But, if he were to have, as you said…a 'look,' it would be something luminous or even burning. You could not see it. It would be too bright, the power too potent. Nothing can contain his complete magnificence."

We neared the long line of others waiting for their acceptance into heaven. We weren't heading straight toward it but rather to the right, where a small gate was positioned with a cluster of angels guarding it. Was this the VIP entrance or something? The angels at the post watched us. All seven wore different styles of the same white and gold Alaric wore. Their hair was different textures and lengths, yet they all shared the same bright golden locks. Their hair was so bright it looked as if strings of pure gold grew from their heads.

I wanted Alaric to continue with his description of God, but as we walked up to the golden-haired guards, he grew quiet. They were smiling at us but looked anything but harmless. Each had a weapon attached by a belt to his side. Two had swords and four had steel nunchaku. The seventh, who stepped up to Alaric first, held a circular pancake object with knives sticking out of it, attached to a small chain.

"Alaric!" He smiled and reached for my angel.

Alaric released my hand and embraced each of these golden-haired warriors in turn. I saw his arm muscles flex as he grabbed them and allowed himself to pulled close, his hair playfully ruffled. They called each other "brother" and chatted quickly about their plans to go out later on "after duty." An angel with two small metallic poles attached by some sort of chain (resembling the Chinese nunchaku) embraced Alaric roughly and more playfully than the others. I could tell from the way they spoke that they were especially close.

Alaric motioned for me to follow as we walked away through the small gate the warriors opened for us. The one who embraced Alaric exceptionally playfully was walking with us. His features were thick, pleasing to the eye, and bold. The thought of *Viking* flashed through my mind. There was nothing gentle in his face or body; he must have been about six feet five, massive, and all muscle. His golden hair was thick; plastered as braids artistically on his scalp with intricate plaits. This massive angel spoke to Alaric. "You want see those moving pictures at my place. I don't have worship until five Light. Get out at ten. What about it?" he grinned.

Alaric chuckled under his breath. "Of course, Marc. I'll see you at thirty to eleven." He paused as if he anticipated another question. "I must help Jung Hwa get settled first."

Marc glanced over at me casually; I waited to feel uncomfortable, but it didn't happen.

"I…" he hesitated, "saw her going to the pit earlier." His head tilted to the side and he scratched at his golden braids.

"You were not deceived, but God smiles upon her now," Alaric said.

Marc responded kindly and rather submissively. "She's a lucky one." He studied me for a moment then brushed his fingers across Alaric's shoulder before squeezing it. "Later."

They embraced and kissed on the mouth. Raised to believe homosexuality was sin, I struggled to place their affection in a category. Marc jogged back toward the other golden-haired angels. I wasn't holding Alaric's hand anymore, so I reached for it and claimed it. Alaric's cheeks had colored, to my surprise, but I wasn't sure if it was because of me.

We walked hand in hand and I took in the sounds around me. My skin glowed like a tiger-eye gemstone reflecting sunlight. No one noticed my presence, or rather they weren't staring at me. I could tell these souls had been on earth, as I had—they were not angels like Alaric and Marc. The angels were in the form and shape of us, yet they had an aura about them easily distinguishable from the human souls I was seeing. Their eyes were like ours, but the pupils were of a shape I couldn't even begin to describe. Their eyes matched their hair in color but never in shade.

Around me, souls were walking and talking. They spoke different languages, but I must have become multilingual or something, because I could understand them. I'd been bilingual all my life, speaking English and my native Korean, but this was amazing! Who would have thought people talk about what they were going to wear to worship service that night while in heaven?

Huge houses lined the avenue covered in gems, sapphires, and other jewels I couldn't name. Small houses after them were pretty and well kept. On the ground were bricks of gold, and flowers grew in the yards with colors I never knew existed. The large flowers were the color of the sunset just after a storm. Smaller ones were more like the color of the sky just after an early morning

CHAPTER VII : Narratives of the Wind (Short Stories & Prose)

summer rain, right at the moment the sun comes out. I couldn't describe them better than this. We were heading toward a large apartment building and townhouses. We stopped in front of the row of lavender and sapphire townhouses. Three golden stairs leading up to a porch caught my eye. Nearby, a mailbox made of sapphire with a small golden handle twinkled in the light. My name was embedded on it and read, "Uhm Jung Hwa, 808 Psalms 23 Court, East Heaven." I smiled and looked back at Alaric. I was afraid, though, that he'd leave me now, but he remained faithful and unmoved.

Something fuzzy and white neared my feet. I squinted in disbelief and leaned in for a closer look. "Snowpuff!" I cried, scooping up my bunny into my arms and smothering him with kisses. "Oh, Snowpuff! I've missed you so much, my baby! Oh!" Snowpuff died when I was nine years old, but here he was, waiting for me all this time. I always wondered if our pets made it into heaven. After Snowpuff, I never allowed myself the joy of having another animal; I was conscious that it would inevitably die and I didn't want to suffer another miserable depression. Snowpuff was pretty fat now, just like I remembered him. He wasn't much smaller than a large cat.

Alaric placed a hand on my shoulder. "Jung Hwa." His voice was soft and pleased. He was smiling. "Come. Let me help you get settled." With my fat bunny safe and close to my chest, I smiled and climbed the three golden steps that led into my new home. I twisted the gold-plated knob, Alaric's soft footsteps behind me as I entered.

"No key?" I asked. He was about to speak, but I interrupted him. "Never mind. Of course there're no keys."

He took his shoes off at the door. "Every house here is a house of God."

I followed his example, discarding my white shoes. My living room was furnished in colors I would have chosen myself. A silver-lined flat screen was attached to my wall. *I get TV in heaven? I bet there's no Taxi Cab Confessions! I wonder what type of stations I'll get, though.* A soft stuffed couch invited me to sit and watch, and little knickknacks decorated surfaces everywhere. Alaric followed me into the kitchen as I opened the fridge.

"No food?" I asked.

He looked into the rectangular pit. "Although not of the flesh, you can still eat spiritual food. Any food you enjoyed in the flesh, you may enjoy all the more in the spirit. Buy what you will and what you need with your allowance. You'll get it bimonthly. A month in heaven is not a month as you know it, but you will learn this." He pointed briefly to a calendar on my wall above the table.

On it posed a woman in *hanbok*, the traditional outfit of Korean women, but the elegant loose-fitting *chima* wrap skirt and *jeogori*, the short jacket designed to conceal a woman's curves, were in modern purple, light pink and white instead of the deep traditional colors of red, blue, and yellow. Her hair was knotted up gracefully near the nape of her neck with a long thick pen piercing it. I imagined the sensation of the heavy silks against my skin, the safety of hiding within the modest shell of propriety while still being fashionable. That level of feminine power was unavailable in modern America and that had always made me nostalgic for a time long past in my native country.

"This is the time of heaven," Alaric said. "Eternity has no ending, although there is the countdown for when the Son will return to your kind on Earth."

Still gazing at the beautiful lady on the calendar, I had to ask. "So when exactly is Jesus supposed to return? I know about the 'countdown.' It's in the Bible."

CHAPTER VII : Narratives of the Wind (Short Stories & Prose)

Alaric closed the refrigerator door and made his way to the lavender couch with a plop. Snowpuff finally grew restless in my arms and bounced down and onto the floor.

"No angels have the knowledge of that date. There were even rumors that God has not even told Jesus himself when he is meant to return."

"Why doesn't Jesus just ask?" I asked.

Alaric smiled in a matter-of-fact way. "Maybe he already has. But I think after the ordeal with the cross, he would probably never question God again. If Jesus was meant to know, God would make it so." He grew quiet and closed his eyes.

I slipped out of the kitchen and marched quietly up the stairs. The first room I came to was the master bedroom. A queen-sized bed with lavender sheets and a purple comforter filled almost half of the space. There was no large screen in this room, only various empty shelves and a long reflective material attached on the inside surface of the door.

I stared at the bed in disbelief. It was the exact same as the one I had back at home, before I died. It took me over three months to purchase the queen-sized gel memory foam mattress with an intricately carved cherry wood frame. How was this real? How was it that one of my first visions after a car crash was hell? Or, at least that was what I thought it was. Seems I had initially ended up somewhere in between. Anger and resentment boiled inside me for the life I'd never have now. *Stop thinking about it. Stop.*

Sprawled on my duplicate bed, I couldn't help but recall just a few moments ago when I was about to get tossed into hell. I mean, I was a good Christian. I still didn't understand exactly how I ended up dangling from the edge of the pit. I went to church every Sunday when I didn't feel like getting extra sleep. But when I did go to church, I was into it. My family even said grace at every meal. I really want to know what went wrong. Well, I guess things didn't really go wrong, because I was here now. But why?

Alaric had led me through the side-entrance to heaven and to my new home. I should feel dizzy with all these thoughts, but I didn't. Where did I go wrong? I believed in the existence of a Higher Power. Should I have demonstrated it more? What would that have looked like?

Comprehension escaped me. I was empty of the truth and overwhelmed with feelings. There was nothing left but to rest quietly in an afterglow of appreciation for The Creative Power of the universe. I knew nothing except that we all must act upon exploring life's deepest questions. What mattered most was a personal devotion to justice, dignity, and the inherent worth of every inch of our planet. A twofold and twisted coin that was one and the same. I bet God kept this coin in his pocket, flipping it when he wanted to make a point.

I rolled over with an exaggerated sigh. I couldn't help but think about Alaric downstairs and how I had come to be blessed with his presence. Did God send him to save me, or did I save myself? Apparently, it was never too late for anything, even after death.

My bed was ridiculously comfortable. The silky fluff of the comforter enveloped me in the gentlest soothing embrace that my spirit sorely needed. The pit of my stomach ached with empathy for my parents. I was starving for their voices in my ears and to look upon their faces. When I thought about how they must be wild with misery, it made me so dizzy I couldn't will myself do anything except hug the literal comfort of the comforter. Why in the world were there beds in heaven if we didn't have a physical body in need of rest? After lying

CHAPTER VII : Narratives of the Wind (Short Stories & Prose)

in the bed for a while it was clear to me—because the bed felt so damn good—that it was more of a want kind of thing than a need.

By the time I was able to force myself out of the comfort of my bed and walk downstairs to my living room, Alaric was nowhere to be found. I was not as distraught about his absence as I thought I'd be. I was sure he was busy doing his angel-work stuff. He could also be flirting with that tall one with the golden corn rolls, who was not so clearly his boyfriend. I didn't understand how gay was a perversion when these angels seemed to be okay with it. What other lies had I been told? What other truth would I learn here?

Snowpuff, in all his fluffy-white glory, watched me from the couch. The ends of his little round eyes peered at me curiously. I was still amazed that he was here and with me. Years ago when I spiraled into a depression after losing him, I wanted nothing more than to hold him in my arms and nuzzle the top of his head with my nose one last time. Our veterinarian slipped Mom a flyer after I went ballistic when she put Snowpuff out of his misery; I was grateful when my father dropped me off at the Pet Loss Support Group. I must have attended that group for at least a year.

I picked up Snowpuff and held him against me. His whiskers moved as he ground his teeth together, purring. Rabbits purr differently than cats; instead of using their throat, they rub their teeth together to make a similar sound that could also be felt. I settled Snowpuff on my lap and picked up the remote control for the television.

I pushed the power button and waited. My jaw dropped as I flipped through the channels. Each channel was of immediate interest to me. Some channels replayed my memories. Other channels showed the veterinary office where I worked as a vet tech, the daily life of my best friend and roommate, my extended family back in South Korea, and separate channels for each of my parents.

I tuned into the memory channel and saw South Korea as it was in my childhood. Our house looked smaller than I remember. I watched my first steps, my entrance into school, our Sundays at church. My family had always been religious; Christian Westerners came to South Korea just to convert us, and my family was among those grabbed by the new religion. I accepted God into my life back in first grade, officially anyway.

We moved to the United States when I was about eight, my grandparents coming afterward once I was twelve. I was reminded of the adventure I found in moving to a new country, and how surprised I was to find so many transplanted Koreans around us in our new city.

I finished school, attended college, and earned my vet tech certification. Another exciting day flashed on screen as I made the decision to share an apartment with my best friend. My parents installed a GPS app on my phone "to keep me safe" as a condition of allowing me to move out. I was their only child, and they reminded me of it every day. The apartment was less than ten minutes down the street from my parents' house. They were tirelessly strict yet relentlessly supportive and loving. My friend and I had so much fun decorating our little nest. Mom was nearby any time we needed help with a recipe or a cleaning chore. Dad was too impatient to wait for the rental company's fixit man to do the work if something broke, so he would repair things himself and bill them. The memory made me smile.

I halted the channel surfing on a scene of some teenagers driving too fast down a residential street, veering into parked cars and laughing but never slowing down. I couldn't see their faces. They were clearly drunk. My heart sank. This was that Saturday night a month after my twenty-fourth birthday. They didn't even react as my car appeared before them and they plowed into me. Police contacted

CHAPTER VII : Narratives of the Wind (Short Stories & Prose)

my parents after running the license plate on my car, which was in my parents' name. Mom and Dad found me quickly enough without their help. I died at the scene holding my parents' hands. Dad was silent and Mom couldn't stop wailing. Both had tears overwhelming their faces. Just thinking about how they must be coping with what happened made me cry.

When I flipped between the channels of my parents, they were showing the same view. Holding hands, they watched as our preacher read my Eulogy. My best friend was on the program to speak and "Awesome God" was the song the chorus was due to sing.

My heart broke and folded back together while watching my own funeral. It felt good to see my parents' faces, but pained me beyond measure to feel their pain, to see every twitch of their bodies as anther sob shook them to pieces. I saw myself – pale, stiff, and encased in the loveliest casket. It was so perfect. Rose petals and lilacs blanketed me and a shiny silver accent decorated my flawless mauve casket.

I looked past the familiar faces in the front row and scanned the pews. I saw them. The three teenagers who took my life. Though I didn't recall laying eyes on them before, I knew exactly who they were. Each was flanked by a parent; I could tell they didn't want to be there. Snowpuff stirred in my lap. I set him down onto the floor with trembling fingers, my eyes never leaving the screen.

I watched my mother take my father's hand and together they left my casket and walked towards the back of the church, pointing at the three youth and their parents. They smiled with teary eyes, and the pointing hand became an open one. I could see the black boy's father nudge him as he was forced to accept the invitation to come forward. Shortly thereafer the long-haired white girl and her best friend, who was this other girl of mixed racial heritage, were similarly pushed forward by their parents. The white girl's father, a man with short blond hair, fingered something sinister in his pocket. He was not convinced of my parents' sincerity and insistence that they attend the funeral. He was anticipating my family and friends in attendance would turn on him like the assassination of Julius Caesar on the Ides of March.

I winced and instinctively changed the channel. There it was – flashbacks of the police station. My parents repeating that they did not want to press charges, to the surprise of the police chief and everyone else. The families of the teenagers were in utter disbelief and pleaded to let them "do or give" *something*.

"Come to our daughter's funeral, please. Honor her. Help us celebrate her life."

My bottom lip trembled. I couldn't tell if I was angry or frustrated or something else. I turned the channels back too fast, skipping the channel of my funeral. Once I found it again, the three teenagers, two pairs of parents, and the white girl with just the one parent, her father, were led up the aisle by my parents towards my casket. With sudden insight, I was aware the white girl had a mother, but her father would not allow her to attend; it was not safe, he said. He attended because their daughter had to. He would protect their daughter by any means necessary.

As the teenagers got closer, their guilt and shame hit me like a hurricane or maybe an avalanche, but it took hold of me until my legs shook, and I sat back down onto the couch. I couldn't stop my knees from shaking. I realized it wasn't just the teenager's guilt running through me. It was their parents' too, all wound up into a tight fireball of intense emotion. My parents looked out into the crowd and wrapped their arms around these kids and their families, making clear to all present that they held no ill will against them.

CHAPTER VII : Narratives of the Wind (Short Stories & Prose)

Making clear they expected the community to do the same. They expected forgiveness.

I wiped my eyes with the back of my hand. No tears in heaven was another lie.

The screen zoomed in on my parents, the teenagers and their parents. Devastated by their actions and inactions, they were drenched in awkwardness as my mother and father pulled them closer together into a clumsy group hug.

The remote control slipped out of my fingers and I reached towards the television. Something filled my heart and I wanted nothing more than to give it to them, to all of them. Compassion cleansed my spirit, and I found enough strength in my legs to stand upright. I couldn't feel my feet move but somehow, I moved closer and closer to the screen. I kept reaching out with the peace inside me until the only thing that trembled was my lips. What I witnessed on the screen was so beautiful to me. Finally, my lips stilled. I shook my head and smiled faintly, pressing my whole palm against the television screen. I heard my father gasp, saw the teenagers and their parents' eyes widen. My mother wailed as she turned her head this way and that; her eyes searching for me as if she felt without a doubt that I was there in the room. Her eyes thrashed desperately as she searched. She found me. We locked eyes through the screen. She cried out my name.

I took a deep, hiccupping breath and responded to my mother's cry with my own gift. I sent her my love and the warmth of the peace in my spirit. Her pale face flushed; her lips smiled and her body twitched as she received it. She and my father would know I rested in peace. The teenagers and their parents would know they were forgiven. My mother and father would never fear death, as they knew I would be on this side waiting for them.

The group hug collapsed onto the floor into a chorus of whimpers and speechlessness. Our minister prayed with his thick lips and held up the Bible. His skin was so dark his large hand got lost against its black cover. The father with the short blond hair stopped fumbling with the weapon in his pocket. He buried his distorted face into my father's shoulder.

When it was over, our family friends, work colleagues, and church friends went to the reception to eat.

I turned off the television and sat still. A mixture of confusion, sorrow, and gratitude filled my heart, but no more tears came. The comprehension that decisions are not always black and white still tugged at my nerves. Decisions are never always this or that. Through His grace, the coin doesn't have to fall on one side or the other, but can stand straight up on its edge, never falling. Always spinning. Defying explanation for all eternity.

I found Snowpuff and nuzzled him once more before walking out the door. I needed to get out and distract myself. Maybe meet some neighbors? Figure out where to pick up my spiritual allowance or whatever it was Alaric had tried to explain to me. The urge to get out of my townhouse was overwhelming. I rushed as fast as I could, closing the gold-plated knob behind me. I stopped after my first step down my three golden steps. Everything felt like slow motion as I took the last two steps, tilted my head as I gazed out in front of me at the elderly couple standing there.

"*Halmeoni* and *Hal-abeoji?*" I asked in Korean. But there was no mistaking who they were or their pure joy in seeing me.

My grandparents stood side by side holding a bouquet of flowers, grinning up at me with smiles that comforted my spirit where I needed it most. I all but threw myself into their arms.

CHAPTER VII : Narratives of the Wind (Short Stories & Prose)

They kissed my forehead, held me and loved me. They would watch over me and take care of me just as they had on Earth when Mom and Dad had to work or wanted a date night. I would be their everything, just as I was as a little girl. The worry about how I would figure out my new situation here in heaven faded like a scent come and gone in the wind.

Gump Graduates

I marched in a slow mechanical line with everyone else, like a bunch of cloned robed kids or mindless zombies. My limbs ached and my fingers went up to scratch my neck. I couldn't help it; I itched.

Alem, my homeboy from way back, smacked my hand down and murmured, "What are you doin' man? Chill out!"

I frowned. "I had to scratch my neck, goddamnit. Don't be pressed, nigga, damn!"

He laughed. "If anyone should be pressed, it's you. You're lucky to even be here, stupid"

I rolled my eyes playfully. "Maaaaaan, you're lucky my mom's here, or I'd give you a beat down right here and now!"

He kept laughing and tried not to draw too much attention to himself. "Shut up and just keep walking, Forest Gump. Your mom probably opened those crusty legs of hers for the principal for you to graduate!" He laughed harder this time, and I felt people glancing at us. But I had to admit, Alem was pretty funny.

I played along, pretending to be mad. "Look, crackhead, don't talk about my mama!" For emphasis I whirled to look him in the eye and snap my finger in his face like some ghetto fabulous chic, but everyone started fussing at me and calling me a crackhead for

CHAPTER VII : Narratives of the Wind (Short Stories & Prose)

messing up the flow of the line. Irritation throbbed in my chest, but the reality was others' impatience was the least of my worries.

A couple of teachers gave us the evil eye for our flawless display of immaturity. Alem just kept laughing, as usual. Whatever; I didn't care. I just wanted to get my diploma and dip out.

We all found our alphabetically assigned seats and sat down. After some clapping and carrying on, we sang songs and a couple of my teachers said their usual crap. Finally, we were told to stand up. I almost tripped over the chair in front of me. Alem was right behind me, and he laughed with strange and exaggerated noises. As we half-marched toward the stage, I saw my friend Tonic.

I had been trying to get with that fair-skinned black honey-bun since sophomore year, but everyone knows she's only into them Chinese, I mean Viet-na-mese guys. She'd always get pissed when I called her friends "Chinese." She'd roll those pretty brown eyes of hers and say, "Not all Asian people are Chinese. Don't be ignorant, Chris."

I'd say back to her, "I'm ignorant for you, baby, so what's up?"

She'd just laugh along with Alem after he embarrassed me by saying I'm dumber than Beavis and Butt-Head on crack, rollin E, and smoking Bud at the same time. Damn. Why's he always have to make me feel stupid in front of buns? I think she liked him more anyway. I don't mean liked-liked, because she only liked Asian guys, but I mean liked him more as a friend than me. So I waved to her and winked, but she only smiled back. It's okay, though. I might not have her, but at least I'll have my diploma by the end of the day.

I felt a piercing jab to my ribs.

"Gump!" Alem yelled at me so that both my rib and ear hurt.

"What?" I yelled back.

"They just called your name—go on, stupid!"

I blinked out of my daze and stumbled onto the stage.

He called after me, "Ha-ha, you answered when I called you 'Gump'!"

Yeah, I thought, as I rolled my eyes to myself, I guess I did.

Tonic Graduates

Everything changed for me on graduation day. I was happy, yet sad. Excited, yet nervous. The only certain thing was I had never felt this way before. I perched in the metal folding chair, hardly still, while both my class president and my principal spoke. The last four years had sped right by me in a blur. I now wore a light blue satin robe past my ankles and a funny little square hat with a bundle of strings pouring down from one side into my eye, while I twisted my class ring on my finger.

Voices and applause intruded as names were read out in mellow and mechanical tones. I found myself standing in line. I couldn't tell you how I moved from my seat over to the corner near the stairs, but I did. Perhaps I floated. Yes, I levitated a few inches off the ground and maneuvered myself over there. I probably looked like a sorcerer, floating like that, with only the tips of my heels poking out from under my long magical robe. I eased closer to the steps leading to the stage. Someone waved to me, but I only smiled in return. My legs and arms couldn't move or bend. I had to have levitated, because legs don't have to bend for you to levitate.

About to walk across the caramel-colored stage, I thought about people who didn't make it this far. I stared at the many others embarking on this journey with me. I blinked; this wasn't actually the ending of anything at all, but the first step in a weeding-out process I'd have to go through for the rest of my life. My view on life changed. Nothing would be simply given to me—I had to earn it as I did this diploma and keep going from there. My legs finally bent and I walked across the stage. In actuality, the line would always keep going. It was important to keep going; it was important to not stop. The line would have kept moving whether I walked with it or not.

This realization struck me with such force that I began to cry. I wondered if this was the true reason why graduates cry at their high school graduations. Was I the only one who masked these feelings by saying, "Oh, it's only because I'll miss all of you so much!" when my tears were much thicker than that statement alone?

Death after the First Era: Cause and Consequence

My fingers trembled as I scrolled through my black smartwatch. I inhaled deeply as beads of sweat collected on my brow. A one-eyed, blind bird with a deformed beak and tail landed above me on a twisted tree branch. The bird shook its tail feathers and flew to perch on the examination building's glass roof. I stepped back from the cliff and sniffed. There was nothing but death at the bottom of the canyon. No fence blocked the canyon's dangerously steep edge, and animal and human remains were strewn on the canyon's floor.

I turned and walked quickly toward the examination center. I tapped my smartwatch and tilted my head to the side.

"Yes, Nori?" Mom's voice spun out of the device.

"Mom. Just got here. I'm standing outside." I cleared my throat, leaned against the examination building, and propped up one foot.

We were silent for several moments.

"I know you're capable," she said. "We can't afford for you to fail a fifth time, please. Don't melt when you get to the question on Africa. This exam is too expensive. We can't…"

I shifted from one foot to the other as Mom's voice trailed off. I imagined Mom chewing on her paintless dark-brown lips before pursing them together. Her dusky, sharp brown eyes glinting in disapproval. Eyes so powerful they could stare down a lion. Mom's hair was so thick and tight that she kept it no longer than a manageable two-inch halo of fuzz around her head. She was beautiful, strong, and fierce like a leather whip made of rose petals.

"Especially with Mama's health condition," Mom continued.

"I know." My chest tightened and my lips trembled. "I feel good about it this time. I didn't *melt*. I don't understand what happened. That's the only question I faltered on. But it shouldn't have cost me the whole exam. I swear; I know this material."

"Good. You said the same thing the last four times, though. You need to start your master's program. Next step—the PhD admittance exam."

I laughed nervously. "One step at a time, Mom. I'm still not sure if I want to go the medical route versus the PhD."

"I know, I'm just—"

"This is all I've ever wanted to do. You know that." I frowned. "I'm going to pass this exam if it kills me. You know this is what I'm meant to do with my life. There's nothing else…you know what I mean?"

"I do. It's your calling. I'm proud of you. So stop messing around and get it. You can do this. You have to."

"Hold on. I'm getting a call on the other line. It's Mama."

"Go ahead and take her call. Call when you're done with the exam."

"Okay, will do."

CHAPTER VII : Narratives of the Wind (Short Stories & Prose)

"Bye, sweetheart."

I tapped my watch's face. "Mama?" I smiled.

"Hi, baby! I wanted to catch you before you started." I could tell Mama was forcing her voice to stay positive.

"Yeah. I'm outside. About to walk in. Just finished talking to Mom."

Mama mumbled in affirmation. "I know you've got this. Do your best and you'll be fine. If the worst happens, you can always take it again. It's offered every six months, right?"

"I know," I said, my voice tentative and low, like a snake not sure if it wanted to bite.

She sighed with an upbeat tempo.

I bit my tongue. I couldn't help but remember the last time I failed. Even after six months, I hadn't been able to concentrate on studying because I had been so worried about Mama's health issue. The last thing I wanted was to make Mama feel guilty about the failed exam.

"Baby?"

"Yes, Mama, I'm here."

Mama was always there. When I scratched my knee, Mama was there. Mama never missed a parent-teacher meeting. Unlike Mom, Mama was a petite woman with wavy light-green hair and grayish-green streaks that bounced with each step, like a weeping willow tree in the wind. I got my petite frame from Mama's side of the family. In contrast, my flawless skin, lips, and eyes were all from Mom's side—skin and lips so beautiful that makeup would make them less attractive if I was at all girly. As a non-binary person, I preferred to remain natural.

I didn't know the details, but Mama gushed excitedly about how Mom carried me in her womb for the first few days before I had been transferred to Mama, where I implanted fully and grew a placenta. Then Mama carried me until I was born. Medical scientists called this method "effortless IVF." During this procedure, egg and sperm cells had been created using skin cells and other DNA from Mom and Mama.

"I love you. Just remember what the tutor said: When it gets to the part about Africa, don't look longer than you have to. Look away and answer the question. You can do it."

"Thanks, Mama. I've got this. Got to get inside now."

My watch phone beeped with a message from Professor Cato.

"All right, baby, take care."

"Will do. Love you."

I checked the message.

Tried to call, but your line was busy. It's important that I speak with you right away.

"Respond to Professor Cato," I ordered firmly. I paused before the watch phone beeped. "Hi, Professor Cato. I'm so sorry, I'm about to walk in, and if I don't right now, I'll be late. Call you right back as soon as I'm out."

The words appeared on the screen. "Send," I commanded. I couldn't have asked for a better, more supportive sponsoring professor. Despite

CHAPTER VII : Narratives of the Wind (Short Stories & Prose)

me failing the exam so many times, Professor Cato was convinced I would pass. She encouraged my love for the planet. The way her brows fluttered when she snapped her fingers made it clear she had always been determined to help me fulfill my life's purpose. A holy purpose to make the world a safer place. A place more respectful to the environment and Earth. I fought the urge to return her call. It would have to wait.

I straightened my shoulders, pulled my short, curly dark hair into a frizzy ponytail, and walked inside.

"Just walk on through." A smiling, balding man tipped his hat with a toothless smile. He motioned to the body scanner. I had seen this man the previous four times I'd taken the exam. He was also chatty with me, and it helped calm my nerves.

I walked under the thin pole that blinked blue and yellow and immediately held out my wrist for the balding man to see.

Solar-powered artificial illumination shined down from thin tubes secured to the ceiling. A cool breeze drifted through the large open windows to the delight of the thin hairs on my arms.

The old man held a small machine over my wrist, and a dim hologram appeared.

"We're just going to review this data. Make sure it's correct." He paused and peered closer at the image. "You've been here. You know how this goes."

I nodded absently.

"Looks like you are still Nori Audre. Born July 12, 2343."

"Yes, sir."

He grunted, withdrew, and peered up at me. "Well, lookie here. It's somebody's twenty-fourth birthday. Got plans?"

I tilted my head bashfully. "Depends on how the exam goes."

"I hear you." He chuckled. "Let's see." He squinted and leaned closer to the hologram data. "Education: bachelor's in environmental politics and reform."

"Yes, sir."

"Sex: intersex."

"Yes, sir."

"Employed by the ecology protection branch of law enforcement," he said straightforwardly. "Police officer, going on three years. Good for you."

"Yes, sir. I'm going to start classes after I pass. Going to get an environmental medical degree." My shoulders straightened despite a faltering voice.

"Oh, you going to be an ambassador for the International Council of Environmental Planning and Implementation, then, huh?" He exaggerated the long name with each syllable.

"Or an advisor. Whichever one. Maybe be an environmental physician?"

"Not the most glamorous work. Outright dangerous, if you ask me," he mumbled. "All of that applied sociology and hands-on environmental healing. Dangerous. Dangerous. You aren't afraid?"

CHAPTER VII : Narratives of the Wind (Short Stories & Prose)

I let a soft smile play on my lips. "No. As a matter of fact, it gets me excited."

"You sure it's really for you? Not being gloomy, but this is the fifth time for the same thing. Have you considered getting into another field?"

My mouth dropped. Lips twitching and fingers tingling, I felt like a merciless Earth's tide blown ashore.

"What's your name?" I asked.

The man raised his brow and stood as straight as his legs would hoist him. "Anderson."

"Just Anderson?"

"Yes."

"Anderson." I glared at the man with my Mom's lion-defeating glare. "I have never been able to imagine"—my nostrils flared with my vehemence—"doing anything less...than everything in my power to heal our planet and save lives." I shook my head and let out a shaky breath. "I know there are a lot of things I don't know, but what I want to do with my life isn't one of them."

"Good for you, Nori Audre."

"It's not even what I want to do with my life. It's what my life—*Earth*—wants to do with me."

Anderson trembled visibly. His mouth curved into the most genuine smile I'd ever seen him give in the many times I'd interacted with him at the exam center. I peered at him curiously. I imagined the large man doing joyous cartwheels and backflips.

"Pays well. Good luck with it." He forced his smile down before clearing his throat and shifting in his seat. "Let's see. The data here says Dr. Cato is your sponsoring professor."

"Yes, sir."

"You're all set, then. Sit in the virtual reality exam pod over there." He motioned toward a row of pods and wobbled over to them.

"As you know," he said between each limp in his gait, "this is a pass or fail thing. Your status will appear on the screen after the last question." He grunted and pulled his slouching pants up to his hips. "The high-pitched beep means it analyzed your answer," he said with authority. "A low-pitched buzzer means your answer hasn't been recorded or there's some type of error. Push the button over there if you need help. The green button is for when you're done answering the question. Don't leave the exam pod. If you do…" He paused and pointed his finger for emphasis. "Your exam will end. Gotta start and pay all over again."

The exam pod articulated in a smooth, strong, feminine voice:

"*With the passage of time as our witness, any form of government that through its structure encourages or even supports unregulated exploitation of the environment cannot last indefinitely.*"

"True," I said firmly, the words disappearing from the large, 360-degree screen.

I pressed the green button on my left to notify the computer my answer was completed. The exam pod responded with a high-pitched beep.

CHAPTER VII : Narratives of the Wind (Short Stories & Prose)

I pushed my bottom deeper into the chair. I sunk into its plush softness and groaned in satisfaction. The only thing good about taking this exam again was the luxurious feel of sinking into the pod chair. The partially enclosed pod was much better than my hard, plastic chair at home.

"What caused the fall of the Computation Singularity Age in 2312? Please explain."

My back straightened, and I sat up. "Exploitation and disrespect for nature...abuse of the land."

I shifted in my seat and squinted. The screen flashed and made clear I had sixty seconds to finish this answer.

"Before the Computation Singularity Age, the goal was to make as much money as possible," I said quickly. "It was a culture of spending. Resources were wasted. The majority wasn't concerned with saving the environment or respecting the earth."

I pressed the green button. The exam pod responded with a high-pitched beep.

"Explain the Scarcity before 2312 and the role of democratic governments."

"In the Computation Singularity Age and the ages before then, there were...thriving democratic governments." I bit my lip and tapped my chin.

The exam pod gave a low, forlorn beep.

"No—no! Go back. I'm not finished."

A low-pitched buzz vibrated against the pod and poured out the speakers.

"I wish to continue my answer! Continue answer!"

Panic coursed through me as I searched for the help button. I slammed my fist toward it but stopped shy when the pod chimed in affirmation.

"Like most governments, democracy had its faults, but with it came great freedoms," I stuttered, still reeling from my close call.

The balding man sauntered next to my exam pod. He tapped his knuckles against it. "Nori Audre. You all right?"

Nodding, I lifted a finger and patted my chest. "I got it now, but thank you!"

The elderly man nodded and limped away from the pod. I squinted and inhaled, as if it would help me stay focused. The screen started counting down from ten minutes and made it clear that the correct answer required more detail than the others.

"Large businesses made the rules they operated by. More of a corpocracy, really. A society where the interests of large corporations controlled economic and political decisions.

"But—" I shifted in my seat. I closed my eyes and inhaled. Information bubbled, then poured like a waterfall. My confidence surged; I could give a lecture to a group of thousands!

"Capitalism," I continued, clicking my tongue. "made extraordinary economies with high GNPs, unlike the authoritative-technocracy government we have today. These capitalistic democracies deteriorated. They lacked the ability to save us from the DFE, also known as the Death of the First Era in 2312 at the peak of Scarcity."

CHAPTER VII : Narratives of the Wind (Short Stories & Prose)

I straightened my back and cleared my throat. "The majority of the world, specifically most Americans, were in denial. Government wouldn't move forward even though the majority wanted to. Corporations were the constituents."

I shifted in my seat when my hands shook as anger slithered to my fingertips. This was why I wanted to be an environmental doctor or ambassador. I needed to advocate, solve planetary problems, and heal the earth. Stop the diseases and stench of death. How could previous generations have let this happen? Selfish fucking bastards.

My eyes darted to the left as a shriek and clap bristled against my ears. Someone had finished their exam and failed. Anderson didn't make his way to the person quick enough. I could only hear the conversation because the test-taker was yelling, otherwise no one could hear anyone else as long as they spoke in their pods. Before I tuned them out, I heard the student claim the computer was faulty and demand directions on how to file a complaint. This center catered to all types of exams, some academic, others social, and some even psychiatric. Maybe the person complaining had some mental disorder?

The computer screen flashed that I had three minutes left. I narrowed my eyes and pressed forward.

"When policy got close to being created, interest groups stopped any progress. Corporations supported elected officials when their time came for reelection. They wouldn't risk profits. Long-term consequences weren't on their agendas. As a matter of fact, it often contradicted their agendas."

The pod gave an affirmative beep. I made it with five seconds to spare. I slouched in relief and glanced out; there must have been at least a dozen others taking exams. Each pod was separated by about twelve feet and an antique-style, hand-carved room divider. The floor was carpeted in a soft navy blue-brown pattern.

The exam pod spoke in its feminine voice again. "*Explain how more profit was gained by marketing pseudosolutions versus cures.*"

I pictured Professor Cato with her straight, shoulder-length black hair and hazel eyes. She typically paused and gazed around the classroom. My mentor was heavyset with almond eyes and thin lips. An intricate Mother Earth tattoo stretched from her neck's right side down to her right arm. She specialized in the history of pseudosolutions versus cures.

"Necessity is the mother of technology," I said. "If you don't think something is necessary or you deny that it's an issue, technology can't help you. Corporations have a history of hiding their savior invention or master solution. More profit was gained marketing half solutions than cures. This has been a proven fact since around the early 2000s. Natural remedies were eventually driven completely out of the market in 2038." I rolled my eyes in disgust.

The computer flashed, indicating I'd provided enough detail.

I cursed with a grin. The pod gave a low, disapproving sound.

"Okay, sorry." I fought to suppress my grin as if the pod was actually able to care. I rolled my eyes and grimaced. Statements flashed onto the screen, imploring me to answer true or false.

The value system of the United States was measured by health, happiness, and sustainability instead of cash flow. "True!"

Given that in the United States of America the wealthy could be cured, curing the rich outside of the Black Market was too risky in exposing the alleged fact that there was a cure.

Definitely. "True."

CHAPTER VII : Narratives of the Wind (Short Stories & Prose)

Pharmaceutical companies lost credibility and went bankrupt as they bullied, taxed, and slandered natural remedies out of the market.

Nope. They won that war. "False."

As long as you are stimulating the economy and creating jobs, it's acceptable to exploit the environment and let people die.

Hell no. "False."

The computer verbalized, "*Illustrate the contributions Africa made to the ecology of lethal disease and contamination as understood by the sociology of environmental politics. Give details of specific circumstances.*"

The screen flashed to an aerial view of drone footage hovering over a group of stumbling, frail beings with deformed limbs and glassy eyes. I immediately turned away and squeezed my eyes shut. I'd seen these images before. The group was the walking dead. A lump formed in my throat. If I was going to help these beings and future generations, I had to pass this exam first.

"Africa got hit hard by DFE, one of the first continents to go into it back in 2278. You need a special permit to visit because it has a higher rate of lethal diseases and deadly contaminations per square mile than any other continent. Africa is a dead zone full of research opportunities."

I nodded and opened my eyes, staring outside the pod in an effort not to look at the images. I caught Anderson watching me. Anderson responded with a polite nod and returned to interacting with an electronic device in front of him.

"Africa got ravaged by just about every industrial country during the peak of Scarcity. The people were too weak to retaliate with terrorism and too resource poor to heal. Even with all the vaccines they give you—if you're allowed to go there—there are many diseases active and growing that we still don't know about yet."

I thought about the many lectures from Professor Cato on this subject. I repeated her words verbatim. "There are three categories of people on the continent of Africa today: the environmental researchers and physicians, the diseased and dying, and the dead."

My mothers had taught me at a young age to be concerned about all people. Africa's suffering greatly disturbed me. My eyes ached with the weight of empathy. Africa shouldn't have been so lost that it wasted away in vain.

"Some country had to be the martyr. An example of what could be. As early as the late 1900s, parts of Africa were ungovernable. Africa is a reflection of our future if we revert "..to disrespecting and otherwise exploiting nature and each other."

The pod gave its affirmative beep. "*Explain repercussions of the tipping point of 2312.*"

I blinked, hesitantly shifting my gaze back to the screen. Relief coursed through me at the realization that everything was déjà vu. Been there, done that. Why the hell couldn't I pass the exam? Clearing my throat, I inhaled and sat up as straight as I could. *Stay focused.*

"The year 2312 was the peak of Scarcity, also known as DFE, Death of the First Era. Everyone was drowning in want, insufficiency, and shortage. Previously, the wealthy had used their power to ease their suffering, forcing the export of natural resources from other countries. The only way these weaker countries could defend themselves was with mass terrorism. Eventually, no amount of money could buy what didn't exist."

CHAPTER VII : Narratives of the Wind (Short Stories & Prose)

The screen flashed, counting down from three minutes.

"Years 2313 to 2323 were chaos," I stuttered. "There was a huge decline in population growth, high death rate, diseases, and confusion. Most women of childbearing age weren't healthy enough to become pregnant or carry a child to term. Live births almost never survived past a few months. Some bought illegal drugs or prescription narcotics instead of food, even when they were starving."

The pod sounded its affirmative beep once more, and it couldn't have come soon enough. I was beyond grateful to be moving on from the topic.

The computer articulated: *"Analysts consider the work that countries outside of the United States do. Assess the meeting of key decision-makers and the Age of Rebirth in regard to how the United States responded to the environmental crisis."*

"Between 2313 and 2323, the whole world as a community experienced its darkest moment. Contemporary sociologists stated that we actually did experience the apocalypse. It wasn't the end of the world, per se, but the end of the world as we knew it. The Death of the First Era of humankind."

I shook my head and resisted the urge to roll my eyes. I'd studied this story for years while in college. Professor Cato had explained the story of "Generation Can-Kickers," the age group forever too self-centered to act. No one deserved to have others clean up after them with bruised knees and aching hands.

Appalled by the mindset of these people, I scoffed. Generation Can-Kickers must have suffered a mental illness. This was the same mental illness that compelled people to record someone being assaulted on their personal device instead of taking action to help. Disgusting.

"The wealthy finally succumbed to Scarcity. Everyone became entirely hopeless. Between 2324 and 2326, there was a grass roots movement of ordinary people determined to do things a different way. This resulted in a mass organization of remaining leaders, sociologists, and scientists."

I leaned toward the screen. "They prepared to create some sort of solution. Things came to light that we didn't know, like the admittance that we are not alone in the universe, although we have seen them, and they have seen us. Apparently, the extra-terrestrials are not interested in any significant communication besides polite small talk and random kidnappings."

I pondered this and recalled my Alien Abstracts and Anatomy course from a year ago. It was the most fascinating class I had ever taken.

I scratched my chin and spoke confidently.

"During these meetings of key decision makers from 2327 to 2346, there was a period of rebuilding toward a common agenda. People calmed down. They put their faith in those who showed leadership, vision, and hope that fulfilled the will of the people. No one wanted to touch any reform based on what they called 'crony capitalism,' which forced us into our situation in the first place."

I cracked my neck, stretched my arms, and rolled my shoulders.

"In 2347, the population increased and the death rate stabilized. People felt secure with the new values. Environmental philosophies were actually enforced. By 2355, the population growth steadied. Now in 2367, we're in the Age of Rebirth. We consume less; for example, a pair of shoes can last over a decade. Experts in our authoritative technocracy make decisions about society. We relax, breathe decent-quality air, and eat mostly vegetarian meals from our local gardens. Our government keeps us in a sustainable economy."

CHAPTER VII : Narratives of the Wind (Short Stories & Prose)

The computer articulated: *"Explain stratification, transferable birth licenses, and consumption as related to Scarcity."*

"If our population gets too low, we make the licenses more lenient by raising the quotas of births allowed. In terms of consumption, we don't depend so heavily, if at all, on what is scarce. Sometimes we're disillusioned about the degree of scarcity we're experiencing. Trees and paper are scarce, but we don't use paper money. Currency gets exchanged with tattooed bar codes on our wrists, and other technological implementations exist."

I shifted my weight and leaned back in the pod. The screen streamed images of plainly dressed women and what appeared to be transgender men waiting in lines to submit to medical clearances for birth licenses. The camera closed in on their faces. My eyes were moist with anxiety and my lips twitched as I watched the faces of those in the line try to feign patience.

"Social stratification still exists. Some pursue careers. Others work from backyard gardens or provide services for small businesses. As long as they're productive and account for hours worked in their communities, everyone receives the minimal allowance on their government currency cards. A universal basic income. Our national health care system works."

"As for worldwide stratification"—I waved my finger at the screen—"there's an international hierarchy. The citizens of the United Nations of Japan, which consists of Japan and a majority of what used to be the smaller countries of East Asia before DFE, enjoy more material wealth than we do here in the United States."

I knew my answer was sufficient but couldn't believe how difficult it would have been to enforce the current value system on someone in the Industrial and Computation Singularity ages of the past. Our philosophy on life was different now. It was a shame it had taken the apocalypse to force us to get our priorities straight.

"Not everyone agrees with the way we've recovered. Some feel that since we're stable, we should revert to capitalism or become socialist instead of our current authoritative technocracy. Our stability at the moment is secure, but the environment is still fragile. We need to be sensitive to this fact for the sake of those after us. Anyone who spreads ill-thought-out philosophies will jeopardize us all. Heretics are taken to rehabilitation asylums. They learn about the destruction caused if they act on their personal philosophies. If they can't understand, we just have to…make sure they keep their thoughts to themselves permanently."

The thought of wayward individuals destroying the delicate peace that took so long to thrive made me sick to my stomach. Under no circumstance should people disregard the earth and future generations. As critical as it was, it should be done compassionately. This was why I wanted to explore rehabilitation as my research thesis once I passed the exam and returned to school. I found it fascinating to discover more humane ways to rehabilitate those consumed with philosophies based on fallacy.

I braced for the next question, but the computer screen flashed, "Exam Complete."

I closed my eyes. In a few moments the screen would show whether I'd passed or failed.

I opened one eye then slowly the other. My bottom lip twitched as my status appeared.

"What?" I whispered, shaking my head as heat rose to my eyes. The core of my soul had been dragged to the edge of death behind a vehicle carrying all of my hopes and goals. My heart bled, sick, hit with a whip of bullets. Everything I wanted in life burned and hung from a tree grown from the expectations of my family and other loved ones. *This isn't happening!*

CHAPTER VII : Narratives of the Wind (Short Stories & Prose)

I eased out of the exam pod, stiff and anxious. My hips ached and my butt throbbed from sitting for so long despite the comfort of the pod. This whole ordeal had lasted a few hours.

Anderson nodded to me as I approached. "Hope you did…" He paused as he looked me up and down. "Come on now, here—yes," he whispered gently, guiding me. "Right here. Yes, sign out."

I held my wrist over the scanner and nodded. I didn't have the strength to hold back my tears.

"You going to be all right, Nori Audre?"

"There's no way out." I shook my head with glazed-over eyes. "I'd rather be dead than live without passing this exam."

"Giving up?"

I shook my head again. *No.* "I'm accepting the end. Done my best five times over. It's just not good enough. Earth is better off without me." I wiped my eyes with the back of my sleeve. "Goodbye, Anderson."

Before Anderson could answer, I turned and moved away. My body exited the exam center on autopilot.

I looked at the smartphone and saw the multiple messages. Mom, Mama, and a few barcodes I didn't recognize. All were asking how I was and if I'd passed.

Peering closer, I fought to keep my wrist steady as the adrenaline slammed down my veins to the tips of my toes. I spotted a large rock overlooking sparse blades of grass and gravel near the cliff. After stumbling toward it, I sat my rear on the boulder. The granite pressed back in stark contrast to the padded exam pod. I trailed my fingers along the rough surface as I looked out.

A few yards away, meticulously planted rows of crops swayed with every gust of the wind. Upon further inspection, I concluded it was a large community garden open to anyone who wanted to work or harvest. Clusters of thin, scantily-clad bodies with weatherworn faces dug mercilessly into the soil with large baskets at their sides. At any moment, the light breeze could easily knock over one of the thin croppers.

A rough indentation played against my fingertips, as if something has been carved into the boulder. As I stood to get a better look, my wrist phone rang, startling me. Through a fit of tears, I clawed at the wrist phone until the band broke. I tossed the thing as far as I could throw.

A small herd of golden-brown goats grazed quietly. Their shaggy bodies had thin, limp extra limbs growing out of their backs. Those that didn't have extra limbs either had two saggy faces, one large eye, or disfigured lips that didn't cover their teeth.

I tensed at the sight of the mutations and released a shaky breath. I paced before returning to sit on the large rock. Head tilting to the side, I bounced down from the boulder. I took a step back and examined the rock to find where my fingers had dragged across the boulder's indentation. Finding it, I leaned closer. I could barely read it because my eyes ached.

"The simpler we make our lives, the more abundant they become. There is no Scarcity except in our souls. Sarah Ban Breathnach," I read aloud, trying the unfamiliar surname a couple different ways.

CHAPTER VII : Narratives of the Wind (Short Stories & Prose)

Shaking my head, I walked toward the edge of the cliff. I wanted to be abducted by aliens; hop into a spaceship and leave Earth. Gone. What did I do for Earth to deem me unworthy to serve her? Why has she forsaken me? Hyperventilating, shaking, and ready to end the pain, I counted: *One. Two. Three.*

A shock jolted me as a biting grip yanked me, pulling me mercilessly away from the cliff's edge.

"Anderson?"

He turned me around to place himself between me and the cliff. "We can't have any of this nonsense, Nori Audre. Come on." Anderson motioned toward the exam building and walked me father away from the edge before letting me go.

I shook myself out of his grip and glared at his legs.

"What?" He tilted his head with a sly smile.

"Your limp." I lifted up my shirt to wipe the tears and sweat from my face. I looked at him in disbelief.

"It was a disguise. I have teeth too." He removed a handkerchief from his pocket and pulled something from his mouth, revealing a set of handsome teeth.

Wincing, I shifted my weight from one foot to the other. "Who are you hiding from?"

"The same people who hacked your exam so you couldn't pass."

Numbness spread from my center to my fingertips, followed by a pounding, angry heart. "What?" I whispered.

Anderson motioned to the boulder. I refused the invitation to sit.

"What's going on? Who's trying to screw me over? Why?"

Anderson held up his hand. "Calm down."

"Like hell I will. This is my life. Everything I ever wanted. Who the hell is doing this to me?"

"The Heretics. They want to reincarnate 'crony capitalism.' We can't let that happen. You know that. They don't want people like you to pass the exam and do anything that could stop them."

"You don't know me."

"We've been watching you."

I shook my head in disbelief and laughed nervously. "This isn't real."

"This is the fifth time you've passed the exam, but the computer failed you. Since you were born, you wanted nothing but to serve and protect the earth. Not only are you intersex, but you have the heart required for the dangerous path ahead."

"What are you talking about? I know you have access to my records. That doesn't mean anything. What does my sex matter?"

"You are more special than you'll ever know." He paused, taking in his surroundings before lowering his voice. "In all your studies, have you ever wondered why—when the earth and the people on it almost completely died off—the hermaphroditic plants and animals like worms, snails, and barnacles never faltered?"

I raised my brow and grimaced. "No."

CHAPTER VII : Narratives of the Wind (Short Stories & Prose)

Anderson stood from the large rock and crossed his arms. "Like the bearded dragons who reverse sex, the intersex Pacific spadenose shark, and the male clownfish who can change sex when their female dies, intersex humans have a special place in Earth's lineage of sex-fluid beings."

"What are you trying to tell me?"

"Don't you see, Nori? You and the intersex like you are pure." He shook his fist. "Pure!" Anderson peered at me. "When mammals evolved from therapsid reptiles and specialized into male and female, they became an abomination. The same happened to dinosaurs and birds. Divided, weakened, doomed to become obsolete. Intersex is the natural order. We were never—never," he repeated sharply, "meant to be one or the other. Since animals mutated into two separate sexes, everything has gone downhill. No more balance. Humans are a weaker species because of it. Yet, because of your natural intersex status, you are closer to the natural order of the world. Closer to the earth, for that matter."

I turned away and grimaced again before shifting my gaze back to Anderson.

"You've studied biology," he said. "The process of meiosis, to create gametes, makes four haploid cells every time, each one different, yet the female body only develops one of these four to become an egg; the other three die. What power chooses which of the four to be an egg? What is the determining factor? Given that all the cells in the body have all the same DNA, the only cells that cut some out are the haploid products of meiosis. This is where the editing happens, where the natural order has been perverted to favor only the sexual dimorphism of male and female. By creating gametes from ordinary cells, this edit is subverted. Intersex genes are allowed to do their job. The natural order is returning."

There was no arguing with him. No point in going back and forth with a madman. I didn't know what was true and what was a lie. All I knew was everything Anderson was saying was rediculous. It was also possible, perhaps even probable. All of it was better than throwing away my life and feeling helpless.

"Your ability to harness the universe's power and Earth's energy is much more potent than that of single-sex people. You are special. You are who we were always meant to be."

"Huh?"

Anderson dropped his arms to the side and stood close. "There's a war, Nori. Things look peaceful, but there are battles going on. All over the world. Heretics are fighting to get back to the past. We've got to protect Earth from what we know will happen if 'crony capitalism' takes over the government again. We can't let big business become the constituents and the common people the helpless bystanders. Never again!"

I nodded. "Who are you?"

"I'm a soldier. In the war. Heretics are using technology to destroy us. We're discovering the inherent, natural power of the earth is more powerful than any technology humankind could create. At least we hope. If we fight technology with technology, we probably have a fifty-fifty chance of winning. That's too great a risk. We have faith that the Earth will give us the power needed to overcome."

"What kind of power? Because I'm intersex, somehow I can harness Earth's power? I'm naturally more connected to it?"

"Exactly."

CHAPTER VII : Narratives of the Wind (Short Stories & Prose)

I raised my brow, snickered, and chewed my lip. I tapped my fingertips against my elbow in thought.

"There have always been people who understood matter," he continued. "That matter, emotions, and consciousness are at their core, made up of the same thing. Energy. When we understand this energy and the energy of the earth, it can be channeled. It can be commanded through a focal point." He clicked his tongue and cleared his throat. "We have natural electrical pulses that create and connect to the core and spirit of Earth. We are all one. But you and the intersex like you are closest to our original state of being. From how we were at the beginning of time. Our physical bodies are just a projection of our mental psyches. Our psyches—"

"I have mutant powers?" I interrupted.

"No. Every single-sex person is the mutant. We are weaker for it. You have more potential than I ever will."

"I'm willing to learn more." I stood straight and nodded.

"Good." He put his hands on his hips and grinned wide.

I looked Anderson over and smiled.

"There's more, yes—I'm glad you want to hear it. But we need to move forward. Let's go to the local headquarters. There are teachers who can explain and train you. Others like you. Will you come with me?"

I folded my arms and cocked one hip to the side. "My mothers. I can't just abandon them. Is it going to be like the movies? The less they know, the safer they will be? If you want me to just leave them without a trace, that's where I draw the line."

He tilted his head. He relaxed his arms and after a long pause and gazed away toward the cliff. "On the contrary. Once we get you better acquainted, we need to go to your mothers. They are intersex. They can help the cause."

"No, you're mistaken," I said confidently. "I know Mom is, but Mama..."

"We know both your mothers identify as female and that yes, your mom is intersex. And the full truth is that your other mother is intersex; she just doesn't know it."

"I don't believe you," I said under my breath.

"It's true," he continued gently. "Her parents weren't comfortable with...you know how some parents are when the doctors get together and decide to play God with their scalpels and biases? We've seen the records. We hope to tell her, if you agree to work with us and join the cause. You know almost all intersex children are born to single-sex parents, but you, Nori—the child of two intersex parents—are truly miraculous. You're the only one we have been able to find with two intersex parents who also has the heart to fight this sacred war. You are the purest of the pure. The strongest of the strong."

My jaw dropped, and it seemed I was in a dream. Surely, then, he knows I'm the result of IVF. Doesn't that make it different? Regardless, Anderson definitely knew how to talk a good game, and his words filled the void I'd felt at the exam center. Was this the truth? There was nothing left to do but follow Anderson and continue to discover how to fulfill my purpose, if indeed this was the way.

"Before I came out here, I called my colleague to meet us a few feet yonder, in hopes you'd agree to come with me. They are probably here now, waiting to take us to the Lair."

CHAPTER VII : Narratives of the Wind (Short Stories & Prose)

"Lair? This does feel like a movie." I chuckled hesitantly, following Anderson to the vehicle waiting area. Dried grass and gravel crunched under my shoes. The wind picked up and swatted gently at my eyes, causing me to blink as I maneuvered closer to the street full of vehicles.

"You know, Nori," Anderson said, "in the most ancient of the ancient times, there were stories told of pharaohs. One of them, Cleopatra, is said to have married her brother. Incest, they called it. But the records were incomplete and altered after enough time went by, just like the books in the ancient anthology that many still recognize as the Holy Bible."

I nodded, listening closely.

"The truth is she did not procreate with her brother. She *was* her brother. Cleopatra was self-fertilizing. She bore children asexually, without external intervention."

Yeah, right! I scoffed. I gagged as the idea lodged in my throat like a foreign object. Anderson's words were absurd and fascinating all at the same time.

Damn, if I wasn't an optimist at heart. Every fiber of my being had never ceased believing what could be, especially if it meant helping others. In the recommendation letter required to sit for the exam, Professor Cato had described me as "uncannily observant, trustworthy, and committed to their goals." It was true. Despite wanting to help as many people as possible, I was also an unapologetic introvert, able to be around others for a limited amount of time before desperately needing to recharge in my own peaceful solitude.

Every person was unique and special, in their own way. Every person, just as Mother Earth herself, had inherent worth and deserved dignity. Justice, equity, and compassion had to be our religion.

Peace and liberty our daily meditation. A free world where truth was so clear everyone could see through lies and stealthy attempts at dictatorship. Where every voice cut through the waste. Where these voices cleared away lies like the magnificent trees that trapped dirt and smoke from the air, absorbing poisonous gasses only to continue blessing and serving us with their sacred gift of lifesaving oxygen.

Anderson stopped and looked into the distance. Our escort hadn't arrived yet. "Speaking of that ancient anthology, the Holy Bible, there's a folktale called The Virgin Mary. You know, the so-called mother of Jesus?"

"Yes, I know. My mothers told Bible stories to me at bedtime here and there, along with the story of the turtle and the rabbit and other folktales."

"Well, for some they still see it as gospel. The Bible finally includes all the books that had once been removed. Like the Dead Sea Scrolls and other forbidden scriptures. Except one. Only one of the scriptures still remains forbidden. After so much time has passed, people still fear its implications. It talks about humans being created initially as intersex. That a rare handful who were even more like God were biological hermaphrodites, which is an impossibility today, as far as we know. They were called the Precious Devine."

"Yes. When God created Adam, he was already perfect. Eve was for company, not procreation."

"No one takes that seriously." Scowling, I stopped in my tracks as if I wouldn't walk any further.

"Now you do. And those I'm about to introduce you to do." Anderson paused his stride as well, challenging me with his eyes. "Just think about it." His voice was coarse with authority. "What some call the higher power—or God or Mother Earth—is inherently

CHAPTER VII : Narratives of the Wind (Short Stories & Prose)

male, female, and all things in-between or around." He waved his arms, gesturing with his hands. "We are her. In her image. Created of her energy. My point with Mary is that there was no 'immaculate conception.' The truth is, Mary was one of the Precious Divine; self-fertilizing. And like the beautiful flowering plants God created that reproduce within themselves, Mary too was a sacred flower of God, conceiving Jesus without the help of anyone but herself—herself and her divine spirit connected to the earth and the ultimate higher power. She bore Jesus of her own seed."

"This is the most interesting thing I've heard my whole life," I admitted and restarted my stride. "Besides what I learned in my alien abstracts class."

Anderson laughed and kept pace with me, slowly including his false limp in his gait as we got closer to the exam building and reached the vehicle waiting area. He paused, waving to the escort lounged in the back seat of the self-driving, worn-looking vehicle pulling up in front of us.

"I'm looking forward to giving you the full history. But know this: we need you. Earth needs you. We have sensei who have been able to do the things I've said. People who harness their connections with the earth. Create fire from their own hands with Chi. Defy gravity. Command the wind and the sea. Hold lava in their palms and move a mountain with the flip of a wrist. These powers are immense. All natural. The only thing that can stand up to the technology we're up against. Once we split into two sexes, we lost so much of what once was. Now it's being found."

I slipped inside the vehicle. Excitement and curiosity boiled over, making my toes and fingers tap. Heat rose into my eyes with an intensity that made me dizzy. I had passed the exam five times over. My head hurt. I buried my face in my lap as the vehicle shook and burst into speed I had yet to get used to. I laugh-cried as my mind wandered to the days of my childhood, college, and the exam. The memory of being bullied at eight years old on the playground used to haunt me, but now it all made sense.

There had been a lone slender tree in the playground's sparse acreage. The dusty brown trunk and scanty leaves that never fully bloomed had dominated the landscape. It was the only tree the school had on its property. I'd named it Alfred. I used to wrap my little arms around Alfred every day when I greeted it at the start of outdoor break. I would sit against Alfred while scribbling thoughts or reading stories on my electronic notepad. Some days, I would just lean against Alfred while watching others play. When I did feel like playing with the other children, a handful of them would say, "Why don't you go play with Alfred?" before scampering off with sharp, exaggerated laughs.

A hand on my back offered comfort. I shook, startled as I looked up to meet Anderson's eyes.

"Sorry. Just want you to know you're doing the right thing."

I nodded.

Anderson let a few minutes of silence pass before continuing, his voice the softest it had been in our conversation. "We have commandments that guide us, you know? Teachers at the Lair. They will explain. The first, though, is *to honor Mother Earth so that it may go well with you and that you may enjoy a long life on Earth.*" Anderson clicked his tongue. "Heretics who don't honor Mother Earth should under no circumstances enjoy a long life. The longer they're alive, the more damage they do. It's our duty to help Earth get rid of them. They're nothing more than disgusting parasites."

Gratitude, fear, and curiosity tingled across my skin, jolting me with awkwardness. My thoughts drifted from confidence to uncertainty

CHAPTER VII : Narratives of the Wind (Short Stories & Prose)

with each moment of the unsettling ride. As we walked up to the Lair, I felt uncertainty would win. I couldn't go forward any longer. The risks and implications were too great. I couldn't do this. Not yet. In that same moment, the last shred of uncertainty melted away when I was greeted with a familiar face. One of the few people who held my utmost respect. My trust.

Professor Cato, one of the many who had been "watching" me, continued to be my teacher and mentor. Professor Cato guided me as I was indoctrinated into MEB, which was short for "Mother Earth's Bodyguards." She encouraged me when I felt lost. Pushed me forward when I failed. Reminded me what was at stake when I dared to consider giving up. Professor Cato helped me discover a lifesaving lesson—that I must let go of my own strength, as it was limited—and instead leverage the infinite energy from the core of Earth herself for transcendent powers that eventually surpassed everyone's expectations, even those of the Heretics.

Anderson was right about what the future held. I didn't know it as a new member of MEB, but justice would be served. No more "wait and see." The future was created. Held sacred. Protected by me and like-hearted, kindred stewards of the earth. The experience of a lifetime.

I discovered my inherent power. Friends became family. I met and fell in love with my soulmate in the midst of tragedy. There was strategy, stealth, and screams. The cost was high, like the tallest mountain where air is thin and clouds rest in the sagging breast of the sky. The pain was immense—as the debilitating agony of inhaling lava's black smoke burned both Heretics and innocents from the inside out. Lives were lost in a hailstorm of slamming stones and fire like the divine judgment passed on Sodom and Gomorrah. Peace was eventually embraced in the arms of truth, stabbing fear in the back like an anguished, narcissistic lover.

Heretics were burned alive in the sky's merciless lightning. They repented through tears. Earth's seas drowned their begging tongues as blood slithered down shaking legs to the tips of their bruised toes, quenching the thirsty soil of the earth. To onlookers, it appeared as a blood sacrifice offered to Mother Earth with as little mercy as the Heretics had given her when they'd defiled her like brutal gang rapists when they pillaged her most intimate, sacred spaces.

In the end, everyone learned that defeating Earth was forever impossible. She was too wise and full of love to tolerate indefinite abuse, or the mere threat of it. She drew the last breath from her enemies by exposing them to her elements. Her indifference was deadly and her deliberateness utter disasters for the foolish who sought to tame her. Her inner power was as infinite as there were stars in the sky. She continued to be underestimated, which helped her unequivocally secure her rightful place as God over humankind.

The Shrine in the Forest

There's a shrine in the forest and it's calling my name. My heart aches for escape and my flesh steams in the forest surrounding me of massive plants and heated fog, like an organic tropical sauna. I stretch my arms and push at the thick branches. They are dark brown with specks of white. One step after another, I walk and stumble. I don't know where I'm going, but my soul is taking me there.

A friend once told me the shrine was made of gold; another said it was built by the stones of love itself. All this rests in my mind's eye as sticks snap under my booted feet.

The soothing trickle of sloshing water is ahead. I push through the brush to find the muddy shore of a lake. Eyes squinting, stinging, I tear my arm across my lashes, collapsing onto my hands. I crash onto my knees at the edge of the lake. My head is like a magnet, the water attracting it like iron. My eyes open underwater; stillness. I gaze within the lake, letting my arms reach out. The rocks are smooth and green; they are purple, red, and blue. I scoop up a handful, and then the water releases its hold on my head. I blink, pushing away the water running into my eyes.

These stones look delicious. Like candy from the pockets of the children of gods. I slip a blue rock into my mouth. It melts. Fresh and sweet, as if the sky were sprinkled with sugar just before a thunderstorm and I ran my tongue against it. My lips curve upward, and I eat another sugary stone. I eat a morsel of the sun's syrup and the sweetness of chocolate's cousin. My shirt is wet. I am bursting through it. It doesn't matter here; I am alone.

I drink the crisp flavor of the lake once more before climbing to my feet. My knees are muddy and I don't bother to wipe them. The sticky coolness is welcomed. I am already soiled and much too hot. I should have rubbed the mud all over my body, but I'm walking again. My long auburn curls are sticking to my face and my arms. A sound I have never heard before draws me through the forest. I slow my pace and twist a few branches away from my eyes. I see knowledge. This is the shrine; I know it is. I never expected to hear this, to see this. In awe, I turn the page.

Storm of Roses

The roses came down, and they blinded me. The petals rained onto me with soft kisses and became a second skin. They became a second soul. They became the well-wishes of someone who had loved me. They contracted between my toes, surging in curls toward my eyes and sticking like bees to a honeycomb. A gentle mystic sang in loud whispers far off against the affectionate weight of the floral rain. Yet past the storm and through the petals I could make out the form of a creature in the distance.

Glowing eyes and disfigured claws peeked from its paws like knives hidden under a trench coat. This beast watched me through the storm. It reached for me, and then the music slowed. The mystic sang again, and this time I understood her. In a voice softer than the petals of these roses, her voice pierced me lovingly and painfully, like a strike of lightning within a kiss.

"In this life, fear hypnotizes our souls. Lost hearts break against empty space. Shall we run or rise? If love is real, might you believe? Impossibility can be conquered."

Every inch of my body went limp when she touched me. I was caught in the feathers of her arms. Somewhere far off, violins played with sharp and quick motions. They played a dreary and frightening tale. I could not see. I would not move, but I could feel the beast watching us. When I finally opened my eyes, I saw moisture under the mystic's lashes. She whimpered, more like a child than a woman. Her face was beautiful and still, void of emotion. If it were not for the blood secreting from her eyes, how would I know she felt any sorrow? These red tears frightened me, but I would not leave her.

The beast tromped toward us, and the claws of his feet ripped into the roses on the earth. The mystic did not flinch when he knocked her to the ground and away from me. My eyes flashed to her listless body. Did this beast bloody my beautiful mystic's face or merely smear her tears? The striking sounds of the violin screeched loudly; I feared my eardrums would melt and ooze out to fall at my feet. My hands shot up to cover them; I even saw the beast shudder from its notes. Suddenly, the scene turned red, as if the mystic's tears were being enchanted from the sky and suckled violently from the trees. Though bloody rain fell, the red roses never ceased. The clouds oozed bloody spit, the gory rain stretching in long, ugly drops as it dribbled like mucus from the sky. Terrible faces engraved themselves as frowns on the faces of the trees. They cried at me in the purest agony I've ever heard or witnessed, like a hundred babies being slapped.

Their eyes frowned like twin crescent moons. They continued to call out in gurgles of anguish as redness bubbled from distorted wooden mouths. A tree reached out at me; I hollered and flung myself from its grasp. I was not aware I had landed right in the beast's path until he caught me brutally across my abdomen. My insides spilt like slop. Every ounce of my being lit up with pain; I screamed. Blood guzzled past my lips. From my mouth dripped blood that blended with the rain around me as well as the sap of the trees. I reached out vainly at my insides. I tried to scoop the mess back inside my wound. Twisting them back into their roots in vain; they were slimy and slipped through my pale fingers. Tired and weak, I sensed the beast laughing me. A thick puddle of blood spurted from my insides, surrounding me like birds to bread. The beast watched. Its eyes and mouth warped full of sadistic pleasure. Shaking knees buckled and broke; I collapsed headfirst onto my own intestines.

CHAPTER VII : Narratives of the Wind (Short Stories & Prose)

Red mucus ceased dripping from the sky. Only the red roses continued to fall. My fingers clutched under me. Someone rolled me over like a newborn in a cradle. No one else except my mystic would touch me so tenderly. I knew it was her, but the roses still came down like oceans from the sky. I could see her velvet burgundy hair and royal purple eyes through the spaces between the petals. She was so close, she was touching me, but I could hardly see her. That is how unmercifully the storm was weeping. The groans of the trees subsided, and the bloody sap oozing from them coagulated and then slowed. My open mouth went dry. Her presence and caress invigorated me enough to pull once more at my slimy insides. I knew she would help me, but her eyes looked disapprovingly, and I was suddenly hit with a vicious shiver of grief because I had caused such a terrible look to alter her face. She gazed eerily past me, as if I weren't there, singing in her mellow voice of gentle waves, "In this life fear hypnotizes our souls. Lost hearts break against empty space. Shall we run or rise? If love is real, might you believe? Impossibility can be conquered. Fear must die in the mind's eye."

As she sang, the depth of her voice filled me. The meaning drowned my soul. I had no choice but to cry from every ounce of my body. She leaned down and licked my tears greedily from my face, but why? The pleasure shook me suddenly, yet I cried out in pain. She had torn my intestines even further from me while I was mesmerized. Why did she pull at the few insides I had managed to replace? I asked her so but she only sang back the words of the previous moments.

I touched her shoulder to coax her into silence. Heat seeped into my fingertips as my anger gathered there and twitched. I did not want to weep again. She might as well have ignored me. She looked at my hand, smiled, and continued her song. She had me in tears again. She pulled the rest of my insides from their source, and I was too weak to stop her. Rose petals squashed under her bare feet without a sound as she stood up and away from me. I watched through the haze of my teary eyes as she traced a square into the earth. She bent down low; her hair fell into her face as she knelt to kiss each point of the square. I watched in fascination as the storm slowed for a moment. Her eyes were of the softness and shade of dark lilac. Her nails were painted with different shades of green, resembling dark metamorphic marbles on the tips of her fingers. They were of a comfortable and attractive length. I could only imagine how I appeared, a lithe glop of a person with my intestines piled in a small stack next to me.

I continued to watch this magic instead of thinking of my appearance. I could no longer see where she had traced the square. Fallen roses covered the earth. The evidence of her handiwork had been disguised. I staggered to my feet, feeling emptier than I had ever felt in my life. I peeled off the torn and bloody shirt from my back. She was smiling at me again, and I had to choke back tears at the beauty of her face. The violin screeched again. Fear blazed in her eyes. She clasped my wrist, and I let her lead me. Together we ran to a nearby tree; I hesitated when I looked at its frowning face. She touched it with her pale little hands, and its frown contorted into a half-smile. We swam to the top of the tree through the ocean of petals together with ease, as the tree grew enforced branches for us to step upon.

Through the storm of roses, the beast appeared and treaded to where we had been on the ground below. I saw the brown beast sniff for us; no, he sniffed for my insides and there they were! He jumped greedily upon them, ripping them with the daggers of his mouth, swallowing them whole. I watched from above with the faint heat of my mystic against me. After a few moments, the ground shook from under us and I watched it break in the shape of a box, which my mystic had drawn into the earth. The beast fell, followed by its low, wailing cry. The tree rejoiced with the others, and its leaves or branches – I'm not sure which – carried us down from its peak.

CHAPTER VII : Narratives of the Wind (Short Stories & Prose)

The storm regressed again; only small delicate sprinkles of warm roses drizzled onto us. My mystic took both of my hands in hers and sang to me. The violins played alongside her voice, and the rustles of the leaves were her chorus. "In this life, fear hypnotizes our souls. Lost hearts break against empty space. Shall we run or rise? If love is real, might you believe? Impossibility can be conquered. Fear must die in the mind's eye. Walk on water or drown in your innocence."

I could answer only by falling to my knees and hugging her skirts. I did not cry. I had something inside me more valuable than the shedding of tears. Only now did I really see her clothes and feel her arms and hands as she petted me. She wore layers of sheer fabric like silk, but even more thin and water-like. The pale lavender freckles scattered along her arms charmed me. I was her yearning hostage. I pulled away from her; the blood of my wound had not smeared onto her. There was no wound anymore. I had been completely restored!

The scene flickered and faded as I came to myself again. Her soothing song followed me as I arose, groggy, from my daydream.

BONUS PIECE

This is one of my earliest pieces. I wrote it when I was in first grade, and I've kept the original spelling and punctuation (as well as all of its errors and inconsistencies) to preserve its authenticity. The names of the characters (Patrick, Jon, Cris, Crisy, and Michael) were friends in my class. I remember reading the story for show-and-tell, using my classmates as characters for added entertainment.

The Patty Story And Jon! And Zon

On day in the Ebony zon patty and Jon patty's frind wore picking off candy trees and food trees Jon said pat let us go to the cool ad pond and get something to drink. But thay did not kowe that Ebony put some girls in the Ebony zon. nat night jon said pat I thot I sow something it Look like a girl pat said I wish! Yeld patty. In the morning the tow girl met patty and jon at the candy tree Jon wisbord to patty I thenk we better run patty said jon has a krust jon has a krust Ha! Ha! O well said the girl's see yu latter boy's eating candy. patty said I think I sode belelv you said patty in a like a girl talk. SO patty and Jon went on talking about the girl's patty sead Jon don't lafe at me if I tell you something OK Jon I think we can mack a frind ship with the girl's Ha! JON! Sorry Pat well let's go to sleep and try to dream about the very very preety girl's sleep tite and don't let the bed bug's bit. the girl's wore takeing a bath in the rerer one girl sead I like Jon he's he's dow! he's nice good and Just nice good. Crisy give me a braek I like patty he's qut o, that's wat I was going to say Cris o, Crisy It's lat let'sget out I left my towl o, Cris I'll sare mine thank's I noww you wod be some yose wen momy had you! SISS. Come on let's go to bed.

In the monthing cras Ebony tree came of help help Patty sead Jon Ebony is comeing Hay! The girl's Jon get the girl's I forgot all about them help! Help! Patty jon ayy! Jon help I have a lot of breck's on my leg help Jon! Patty help I have a tree trunk on my left leg ayy! You have a bad brozz she dus to! Ono! Here come EBONY!! I am Ebony the roller of all the Ebony zon! Stand befor me ney now! I'm scard patty o Just go come on ney! Yes we ney! Yes mam! I am a Queen Ebony now that you people have prod wat you well serd me I shall let you stay is the Ebony zon! So be it you like the girl's So I will let you get marid and the pastor will be Mike Farrol my good frind! So let the weding beGin! Biy my frind!

Dayley brlove in let the people helping sorrow and in ned do you take your man We do jon patty do you take your girl we do you may kiss your brid mou! mou!

BONUS PIECE:

I wrote this when I was in second or third grade, and I've kept the original spelling and punctuation (as well as all of its errors and inconsistencies) to preserve its authenticity. The names of the main characters are taken from my grandmother, Queen Irene Peace. Cats have been my favorite animals for as long as I can remember. I was and still am an avid fan of Bruce Lee and his films; this story reflects and is inspired by those two interests.

The Ninja Cat Irene

Once there was a Ninja girl named Queen. She was the best Ninja in the world. She had a cat named Irene. Iren had a little sister named Peace. Queen taught in the biggest Dojo in the world. The Dojo was famous because it was the best training center in the world for Ninjas, The Dojo's campus was very big. The building had 90 floors of pictures of Ninjas on the walls. But, there was a mean cruel Ninja cat named Irenep. Irenep wanted to be the best Ninja in the world. Irenep was very jealous of Queen. One day Irenep shot Queen six times. Before Queen died she said to her best friend (her cat Iren), "I will pass the honor of the Ninja skills to you," and now the girl cat Irene could talk. She said "Irenep. I'll kill you," "I'll get the REVENGE!" And after she said that, Queen's eyes closed. Queen said "my cat." Then Irene started to cry. "I'll find you Irenep, if it's the last thing I do!" The Irene got her black and red Ninja suit that Queen had been saving up for her. She got the black cat ninja belt. And also started searching everywhere for Irenep in the giant Dojo. Irene had to fight Irenep's helpers. They were good but not good enough!

As Irene fought with anger, she tied up some Ninja cats up with rope and knocked out some of the Ninja cats. Then Irene jumped up to the second highest floor, as usual, to beat up the next Ninja cat. This time this cat looked stronger and bigger than the other cats she had beaten up. The Ninja cat kicked Irene h..a..y..y, O..o.h, y..o..u.. u..o.. u..t..a..k..e..t..h..a..t. Irene kicked the Ninja cat up the wall. And that fight was over. Then Irene Jumped up to the highest floor, as usual.

There was the second best Ninja in the universe, Irenep! "S..O...O you've met your Doom Irene," Irene said. Putting her hands on her cheeks, "oh no! it's the great Irenep! Oh I'm so Scared, save me!" then she fell on the ground pretending she was dead. As Irenep came close, Irene got up surprisingly and started fighting. Irenep blacked and kicked Irene. Irene fell straight to the ground of the giant Dojo. Irene didn't get hurt badly. Then Irene knocked Irenep up the wall. Now they were ready to fight, b..a..m! b.o.n.g! A..y..A.y.y.y I..y..a..! take that That does it! Oh you Imbecile! The sounds of the fight were horrible They were fighting for a few hours. Then they were face to face. Huhu,huhuu.huhuhu.

OK so you're a little hard but I can still beat you said Irenep. Then music of Black Cat came on. Two hours latter Irene won. It was hard, very hard. Suddenly, IRenep got up and ran. I'll get you yet Irene Ha! Ha! Ha! Echoed as she made her escape! Irene would continue to search for Irenep to get the REVENGE!

Note to Readers

Dear Reader,

I hope you enjoyed Storm of Roses: A Compilation of Poetry and Short Stories. I'm so grateful for your eyes on these pages! I deeply appreciate your support. The top three things you can do to support me are:

1. Write a Review. This is by far the most helpful and supportive thing you can do. Amazon, Goodreads, and Barnes & Noble are great places to start!
2. Subscribe to my blog and comment on my posts at https://etarascurry.com/blog/. There are also free stories and poetry on my blog that you can enjoy
3. Join my VIP List! by signing up through my website, https://etarascurry.com/. You'll receive freebies, special offers, free books, updates on my latest stories, and my quarterly *Apatite Books & Café Newsletter*

Thank you for reading and I welcome your feedback. Write to me at etarascurry@gmail.com or Chrysocolla Publishing P.O. Box 4858 Silver Spring, MD 20914.

You're also invited to hang out with me and like-minded friends on Twitter @ETaraScurry and in my Facebook Group: https://www.facebook.com/groups/etarascurry/

Having readers like you is my dream come true. I appreciate you! Stay in touch.

~ E. Tara Scurry

Also by E. Tara Scurry

SPARK: A Story and Poems Lit Aflame

Release Date: July 2020

SYNOPSIS

"It's dark, it's beautifully twisted and I'm happy to have had a chance to read it."
— Madison Drake,
Copy Editor, Content Editor, Proofreader & Beta Reader

"This is a really a strong story, it stuck with me for days after reading!"
— Ryan McDonough,
Millennial Storyteller, TV/Film Writer & Ghostwriter

With a story that tests your resolve and poems that reverberate long after they've been read, Spark: A Story and Poems Lit Aflame presents a raw, unapologetic voice on divinity, survival, and cruelty. Spark is the pre-release "single" from the long anticipated revised edition of Storm of Roses: A Compilation of Poetry and Short Stories.

This is an essential read for curious readers' eager for their first bite of E. Tara Scurry's thought-provoking literary art. Spark begins with its 7,000-word title piece about an abused girls tipping point that forces her to seek revenge by telling disgusting lies.

Not a story for the faint, heed the disclaimer for violence, miscarriage, torture, abuse, and cannibalism. After your resolve is tested, E. Tara Scurry sprinkles you with an insightful selection of sixteen poems that synthesize a deep connection with our actions, choices, and their impact on the world around us.

CRACK OF DAWN (The Vampire Apostles book 1)

A Dark Urban Vampire Romance

Release Date: 2022

SYNOPSIS

Despite being financed by his talented transgender prostitutes, a gritty, crack-addicted pimp unwillingly accepts the help of a vampire in exchange for surrendering his body and crack infused blood to satisfy the vampires own dark addictions. He believes his existence is inconsequential, but Jesus has other plans.

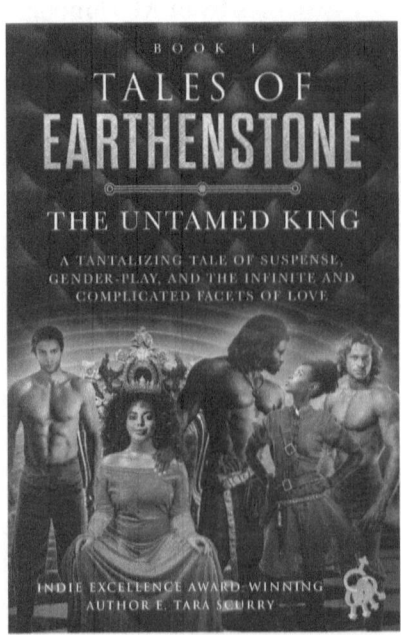

THE UNTAMED KING (Tales of Earthenstone book 1)

Release Date: TBA

SYNOPSIS *Earthenstone*
Amaron VelKoina: The rugged and bold specimen accidently killed a peer with one punch to the heart. He prospered in fighting arts, hunting, problem-solving, and the broad sword. Both feared and desired. As a young man in waiting, he had been kept chaste from women and prepared for becoming a King to a powerful Queen.

Queens of the Realm waited impatiently for him to be presented. Finally, after five years past due, he was formally presented to high society, pronouncing him as a young man ready for marriage. Close to his deaf mother, she let him procrastinate on marriage until enough was enough. Quickly enough, after formal courtship, his mother chose a perfect fit for her beloved eldest son, Queen Xerah IV of Earthenstone.

As Xerah's first husband, he had given her sons and none of the daughters she needed as heirs. It was common for Queens to take multiple husbands, so when Xerah took three more, after their years of marriage, Amaron bit his tongue and held his head high.

Yet, there was something strange about one of the new men in the palace. He was hiding something under those delicate features and soft voice. What sort of man was not excited about becoming a King? Xerah must have chosen him for his kitchen mastery and nothing more; it was obvious he was of the more...delicate and gentle type of men, not good for much else, like the breeding of daughters. He failed miserably at trying not to stare at Amaron's chiseled body. This was amusing. Could prove quite interesting considering Amaron was not a novice at initiating carnal attention from other men. Yet when Floran was not staring, he seemed dejected, paranoid and lost in thought.

Floran, had no choice: Run away or leave her mourning and vulnerable father. She couldn't leave him. Ever. Instead, she dressed as a young man to evade creditors until she could earn her way out of her family's debt. Life took a dangerous turn when she was meticulously chosen for her kitchen mastery skills as one of the three new husbands of Queen Xerah IV of Earthenstone.

Can Floran keep her identity a secret forever or tell it without being killed for deceiving the entire realm? Only when secrets are revealed and love distorts logic can Amaron fulfill his destiny.

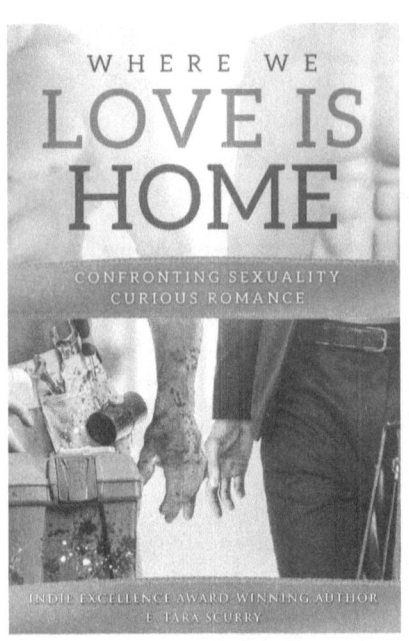

WHERE WE LOVE IS HOME

Release Date: TBA

Confronting Sexuality. Curious Romance

SYNOPSIS

A Latino general contractor and young American lawyer build an unlikely friendship that threatens their sexuality, destroys the status quo, and ignites their most deeply held desires.

HELL'S LOVER

Release Date: TBA

A blasphemous Book of Love. War. Forgiveness. Peace

SYNOPSIS

When an Archangel's world is literally turned upside down after following his abusive lover into Hell during The Rebellion, his lover's true soul mate, Lucifer, is consumed with fulfilling his destiny to annihilate every flicker of God's overwhelming power and love.

ANGELS WEAR ORCHIDS:

A Compilation of Poetry and Short Stories
Release Date: TBA

SYNOPSIS

Diverse and eccentric, Angels Wear Orchids is the second compilation of poetry and stories from award-winning author, E. Tara Scurry.

Beginning with the authors trademark distinctive prose, the first section of the book includes song lyrics and poetry. The second part includes five stories.

"The Cleaning Lady" follows a Vietnamese immigrant baited into a human trafficking ring when she arrives to interview as a housekeeper. She uses her creativity and courage to stay alive and plan her escape.

In "Three Leaf Clover" a workaholic black woman allows the two men she's dating to care for her cats when her boss unexpectedly sends her out of the country for work. Leery and resentful of each other, they eventually find more satisfying things to do with each other than share pet-sitting duties. When tragedy strikes this devoted threesome, a silver lining emerges.

"Pimp My Wheelchair" is a no holds barred dark comedy. It features a conceited wheelchair bound senior citizen and his clique of elderly and disabled friends who terrorize the patrons of Union Station in Washington DC.

"Tomorrow We Die" follows two comrades in arms as they make the most of their lives before facing one more excruciating battle against an opposing army.

In the title story "Angels Wear Orchids", the lead singer of a Neo-goth rock band falls in love with his sassy and hardworking personal assistant, to everyone's dismay, including hers. Being an interracial couple is the least of their differences: he's into scandalous erotic bondage and she wants nothing to do with it. He wants all of her attention and she needs to take care of family who sacrificed everything to support her success. She believes in what's Right and he believes in Right Now. Is their relationship worth the effort? Will their feelings leave them no choice but to give in to each other, despite the odds?

ABOUT THE AUTHOR

E. Tara Scurry lives her life's purpose by storytelling to make the world a better place and give reprieve and joy to those who need it most. You'll find her speaking at events and socializing on Twitter. Irrespective of creating in different genre's, her poetry and stories are always provoking, eccentric, inclusive, and openhearted. She writes about love, social problems, self-introspection, and the divine – all from a sociological perspective. She has gratefully added joy and thought-provoking experiences to her readers for over 3 decades; most of which was before she was formally published.

As a Speaker, she has taught at progressive places of worship, conferences, academic classes, and served as an inspirational speaker at Women's Retreats.

As a Storyteller, she believes her stories impact the world by making it more welcoming and inclusive. That the world is a better place when all feel safe, respected, and comfortable expressing all aspects of our identities. She believes that a whole life can change by one story. One experience can change a heart.

E. Tara Scurry is a graduate of Sweet Briar College and Johns Hopkins University's Carey Business School with a B.A in Sociology, Law & Society minor and a M.S. in Organizational Development & Strategic Human Resources.

A native of the D.C. Metropolitan area, she lives in Silver Spring, Maryland. Subscribe to her blog at https://etarascurry.com/blog/, and connect with her on Goodreads, Twitter https://twitter.com/etarascurry, Facebook, and YouTube.

www.ingramcontent.com/pod-product-compliance
Lightning Source LLC
Chambersburg PA
CBHW022036290426
44109CB00014B/878